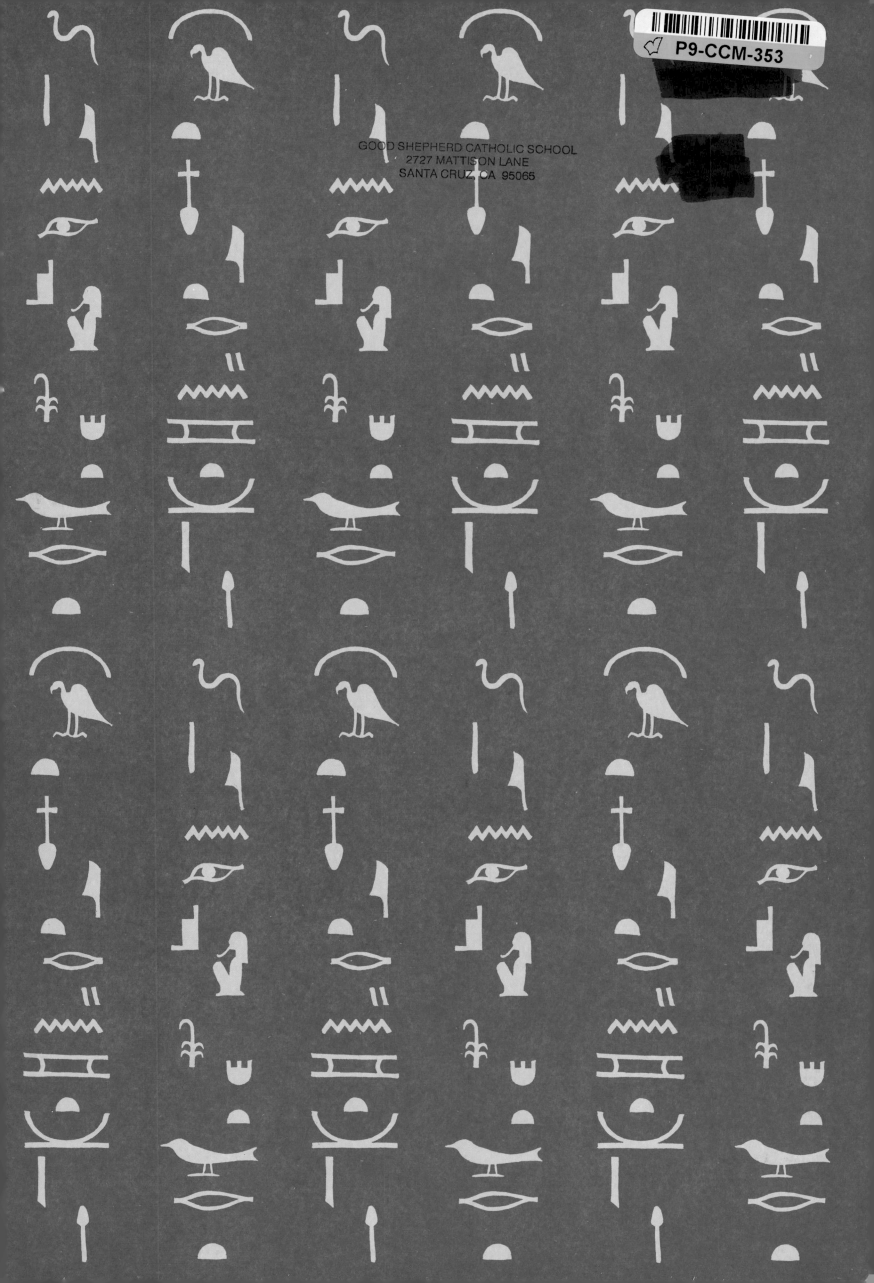

EXPLORING THE PAST

ANCIENT EGYPT

GEORGE HART
ILLUSTRATED BY STEPHEN BIESTY

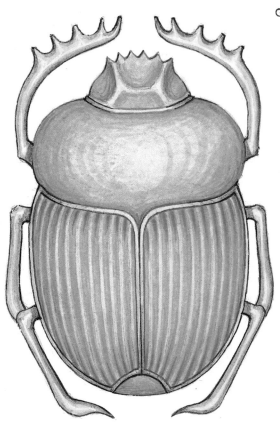

GULLIVER BOOKS
HARCOURT BRACE JOVANOVICH, PUBLISHERS
San Diego   New York   London

First published 1988 by Pyramid Books, an imprint of the
Octopus Publishing Group Limited
Copyright © 1988 by Octopus Books Limited

Library of Congress Cataloging-in-Publication Data
Hart, George, 1945–
Exploring the past: Egypt / by George Hart; illustrated by
Stephen Biesty.
p.   cm.
"Gulliver books."
Includes index.
Summary: Presents an overview of life in ancient Egypt
discussing such topics as the Pharaoh, religion, mummification
and afterlife, the role of scribes and craftsmen, home and family,
and common occupations.
ISBN 0-15-200449-1
1. Egypt—Civilization—To 332 B.C.—Juvenile literature.
[1. Egypt—Civilization—To 332 B.C.]   I. Biesty, Stephen, ill.
II. Title.
DT61.H285 1989
932′.01—dc 19   88-30065

Produced by Mandarin Offset
Printed and bound in Hong Kong
B C D E F

CONTENTS

INTRODUCTION

The civilization of Ancient Egypt flourished on the banks of the river Nile for over 3,000 years. But it had already been dead for 1,000 years when the Magna Carta was signed in A.D. 1215.

This comprehensive book takes the lid off the "sarcophagus" of Ancient Egypt and looks in to see what life was like for the people who lived and worked so long ago. Could you have survived the vigorous training in an Ancient Egyptian school? Would you have enjoyed working as a jeweler or being an Egyptian peasant? Would you have liked the food and drink? You will soon find out when you read this book. You will also learn why the Pharaoh was so special and how powerful his queen could be. You will have a glimpse of the secret rituals of an Egyptian high priest and learn about the legends of some of the gods and goddesses he served. You will learn exactly what went on inside the embalmers' tent, how a mummy was made, and what happened at a funeral.

This book will give you a start in Egyptology. Then who knows? When you are older, you might be telling the world about the royal tomb you have discovered or the ancient town house you have excavated.

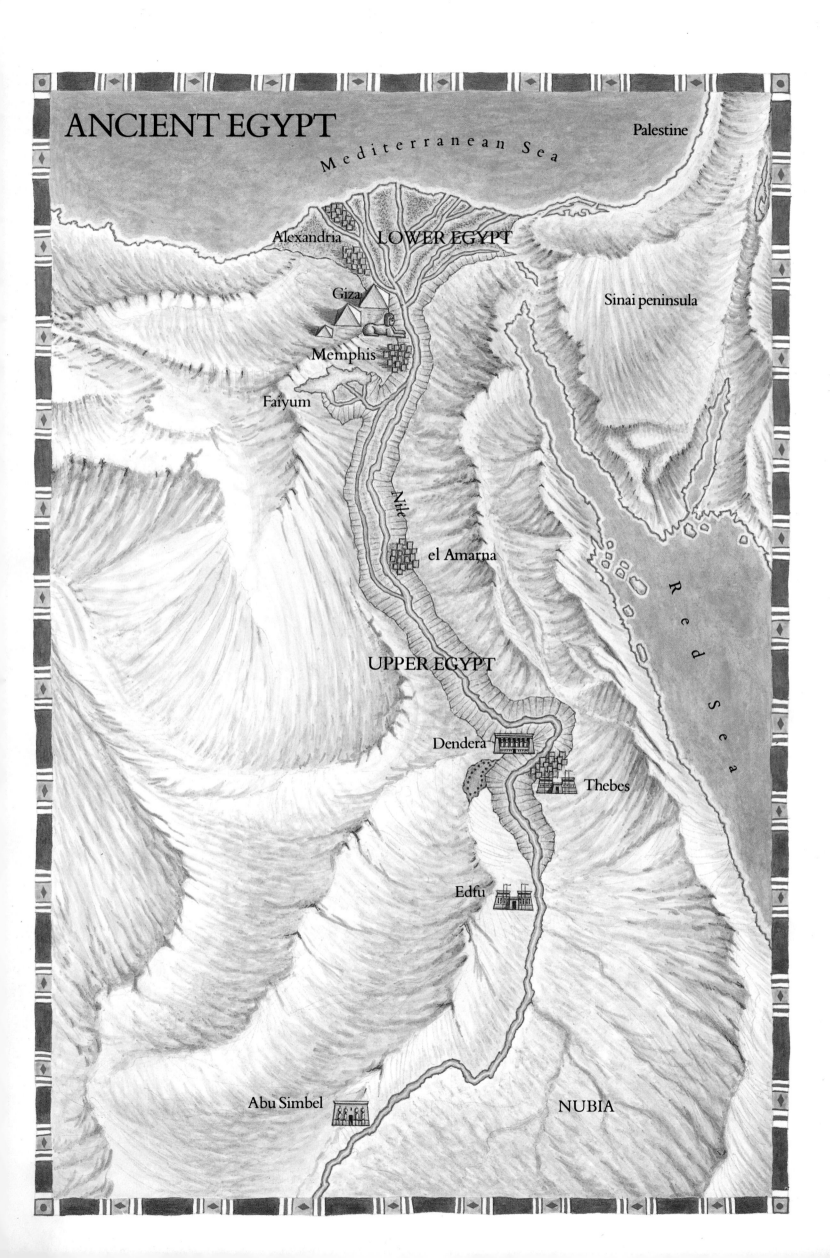

THE PHARAOH

Ostrich-hunting in the desert

Enjoying a game of senet

Tutankhamun's throne

Nubian giraffe

The first Pharaoh killing his northern rival

Rewarding courtiers

Being massaged with perfumed oil

Sailing south on the Nile

Target practice

Vizier's report

Approving a temple inscription

Performing the Jubilee Festival ritual

THE GOD-KING OF EGYPT

About 5,000 years ago in the northeast corner of Africa there was a civilization that we now call Ancient Egypt. It was made up of two separate kingdoms. The southern kingdom, or Upper Egypt, grew along the narrow floodplain of the river Nile and stretched downstream (northward) from Aswan. The northern kingdom, or Lower Egypt, was on the wide delta of the river Nile. This area was full of marshes and lagoons.

Each kingdom had its own chieftain. For centuries, the two kingdoms had fought each other to gain control of the whole country. Eventually, in about 3000 B.C., the ruler of the southern kingdom, King Narmer, conquered his northern enemy, and Upper and Lower Egypt were united.

King Narmer, also known as Menes, needed a new capital city. He founded the city of Memphis, where the old northern and southern kingdoms met. Memphis is the name that the ancient Greeks gave the city. The Egyptians gave it a name meaning "Balance of the Two Lands."

People often refer to the kings of Ancient Egypt as the pharaohs. This word comes from an ancient Egyptian title for the monarch, "per aa," meaning "great house" or "palace."

The Pharaoh was considered to be a god, especially when he was wearing his full regalia of crown, ceremonial beard, and scepters. He was given five different titles, each describing the powers that the Egyptians thought he had.

The Pharaoh in full regalia listens to a report sent by his fortress commander.

The Horus Title

This title is written with an image of the hawk, symbol of the god Horus. In identifying with Horus, the Pharaoh was claiming his right to rule the country. The Egyptians believed that a tribunal of gods had awarded the throne to the god Horus after he and the god Seth had fought for it.

The royal god Horus

The Two Goddesses Title

The two original kingdoms of Egypt each had a protecting goddess who continued to be powerful after the unification by Menes. The north was looked after by a cobra goddess called Wadjet. Her image was worn on the crown or forehead of the king. It was thought that she could destroy the Pharaoh's enemies in battle by spitting at them. The goddess who protected Upper Egypt took the form of a vulture and was called Nekhbet.

Protective goddesses Wadjet and Nekhbet

The Golden Horus Title

This title is shown as a hawk standing on the Egyptian symbol for gold. It strengthened the Pharaoh's image as a god by suggesting that his flesh, like the sun god's, was made from precious metal.

Horus on a collar of gold

The Sedge-Plant and the Bee Title

This title is usually translated as "King of Upper and Lower Egypt." The sedge was associated with the south, while the bee symbol originated in Sais, an ancient northern sanctuary of the goddess Neith.

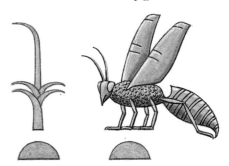

Southern sedge and northern bee

The Son of Re Title

The pintail duck and a disk make up this title. The duck meant "son," and the disk stood for "the sun god, Re." So the Pharaoh was regarded as the child of Re, most ancient and powerful of the Egyptian gods. This was therefore an important title.

Duck and the sun disk

THE GREAT ROYAL WIFE

The Pharaoh was the supreme power in Egypt, but his principal queen also played an important role. She was known as the Great Royal Wife. Her son succeeded to the throne of Egypt. If she had no sons, then her eldest daughter became the heiress and would marry one of the Pharaoh's sons by another wife. This procedure gave the prince a proper claim to the throne.

Queens of Egypt had beautiful regalia. They wore fine linen dresses and held a scepter in the shape of a lily, the sacred plant of Upper Egypt. Over their wigs they often wore a headdress shaped like a vulture goddess, with wings and talons coming down on each side of the head, or one like a Sun disk with tall plumes of gold on top.

Some of the best-known queens lived during the period that we call the New Kingdom, which lasted from about 1550–1070 B.C. The most powerful of all was Queen Hatshepsut. She ruled on behalf of her stepson, who was too young to rule on his own. But she soon decided to take over the government of Egypt completely and reigned as its monarch for about twenty years. She had herself shown as a king and wore a pharaoh's crown, special linen kilt, and the ceremonial beard.

Queen Hatshepsut's architects built a splendid temple for her on the west bank of the Nile at Thebes. Today it is called Deir el-Bahri. When her stepson came to the throne as King Tuthmosis III, he hacked out her name and image from buildings and records, pretending that she never reigned.

Above: *The Queen in her regalia of plumed crown and vulture headdress, holding a scepter of authority*

Below: *The powerful queen, Hatshepsut, makes a state visit by royal boat to inspect her temple at Thebes.*

Hatshepsut's memory became hated by later Egyptians because she had had no right to the throne, and her name was never included in any official list of rulers.

Later, in about 1390 B.C., Amenhotep III ruled Egypt. He chose the daughter of the master of his chariotry to be his Great Royal Wife. She was Queen Tiye. Their son was Akhenaten.

When Akhenaten was Pharaoh, his principal wife was Queen Nefertiti. Some people think that Queen Nefertiti became co-Pharaoh with Akhenaten toward the end of his reign. Akhenaten was not popular, and when he died, his name and face were removed from nearly all the monuments. Queen Nefertiti suffered the same fate as her husband.

Ramses II ruled for sixty-seven years in the thirteenth century B.C. and for part of his reign Queen Nefertari was the Great Royal Wife. She was given her own temple at Abu Simbel. There she is shown being crowned by Isis and Hathor, two goddesses of great importance in

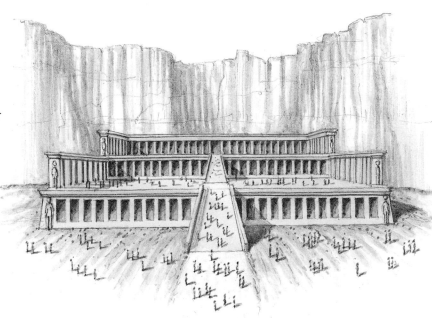

The mortuary temple of Queen Hatshepsut at Thebes, rising in terraces.

Egyptian religion. (Her temple, along with that of King Ramses II, was moved to a higher level away from the area to be flooded when the Aswan Dam was built in the 1960s.) Her tomb is in the Valley of the Queens and contains some of the most beautiful scenes ever painted.

The temple at Abu Simbel dedicated to Queen Nefertari by her husband Ramses the Great.

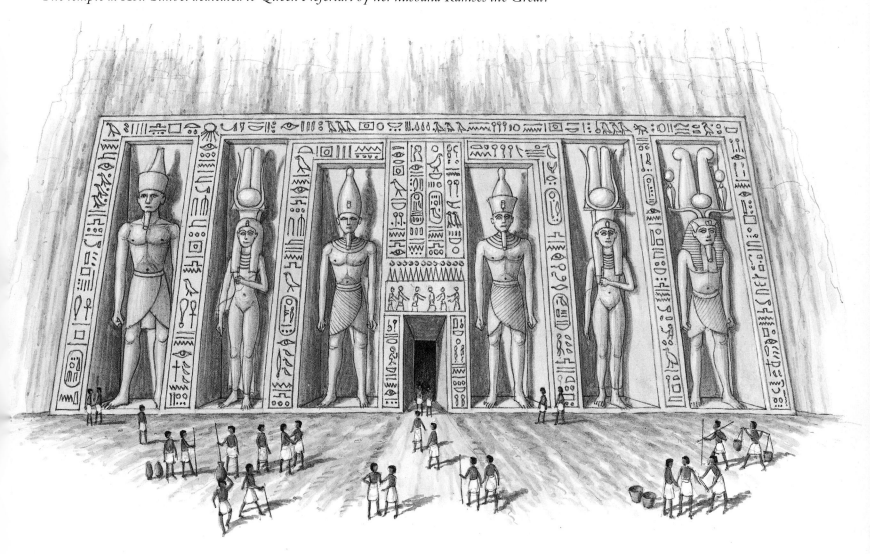

THE KING AS WARRIOR

Many scenes carved on temple walls in Egypt show the Pharaoh destroying his enemies. Sometimes he is in his chariot shooting arrows at the enemy army. At other times he appears superhuman in size, holding captives in one hand by their hair and in the other raising his mace to smash their skulls.

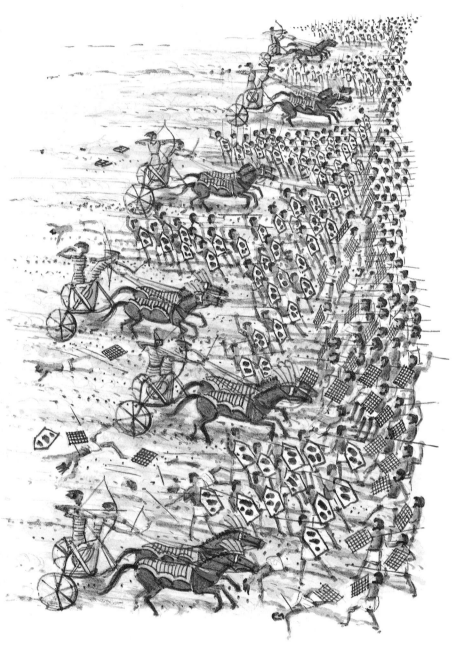

The Pharaoh's army attacks the enemy.

At its best, the Egyptian army would have been very hard to beat, even though the Pharaoh's infantry soldiers wore no real protective armor, just linen kilts and perhaps an upper corselet. They carried shields of ox hide, and copper and bronze weapons such as spears, scimitars, and axes. After the infantry had broken the enemy ranks, the Pharaoh's chariots charged into battle at high speed. There were two soldiers in each vehicle, one to steer the pair of horses and the other to shoot arrows. The bow was made of strips of wood, leather, and horn. In paintings, however, the Pharaoh is shown in his chariot without a driver. Instead, he is pictured guiding the chariot with the horses' reins tied around his waist, thereby showing how skillful and brave he was.

An image of the young King Tutankhamun charging a Nubian army is painted on a chest found in his tomb. He was also buried with a shield that pictured him as a sphinx (with his head on the body of a lion) trampling two slain Nubians. But Tutankhamun only had a short reign, and it is unlikely that he led his army abroad.

Armor and weapons of an Ancient Egyptian soldier

Probably many of the paintings were based on actual events. For example, a scene from the wall of one of Ramses II's temples shows him in his chariot attacking a force of Nubians. And, there is a particular battle that we know of, fought by Ramses II against the Hittites, in which Ramses almost lost his life.

According to the inscriptions about this battle, the Pharaoh was given immense strength by the god Amun and cut his way through the enemy chariots alone. In reality, the Pharaoh's commando force arrived just in time to take the Hittites by surprise and cause confusion in their ranks. Ramses II displayed great courage in battle, but he failed to drive the Hittites from the Middle East. Nevertheless, when he returned to Egypt, the Pharaoh ordered his artists, who were working on his great temples such as Ramesseum, Luxor, and Abu Simbel, to portray the Hittites as having been conquered and himself as an unbeatable warrior.

The most impressive warrior Pharaoh was King Tuthmosis III, who ruled Egypt in the middle of the fifteenth century B.C. In a series of victorious campaigns in the Middle East, he managed to bring under Egyptian control all lands up to the banks of the river Euphrates in Syria.

Above: *On a painted casket and shield, Tutankhamun plays the roles of a victorious Pharaoh charging into battle and a sphinx defeating the Nubians.*

Below: *Ramses the Great, leading his sons, attacks a Middle Eastern army (from a Nubian temple relief).*

13

PYRAMIDS AND THE VALLEY OF THE KINGS

Since the Egyptians regarded the Pharaoh as a god, he could not die in the same way as an ordinary human being. One belief was that his soul flew to the horizon in the shape of the hawk god, to be united with the Sun. Another was that his spirit joined those of his ancestors as a star in the sky. According to yet another view, the Pharaoh descended into the Underworld to rule as the god Osiris.

The Pharaoh spent a great deal of money on his tomb to make it worthy of a god-king and to protect it from robbers. Early kings were

An early royal tomb

Djoser's step pyramid

buried in large low-lying tombs built mainly of mud bricks. In 2600 B.C. the age of pyramids began. The first pyramid was built for King Djoser on the desert plateau at Saqqara, overlooking the ancient capital of Memphis. It rises in six steps to a height of nearly 200 feet and was meant to suggest a gigantic stairway for the king's spirit to join the sun god.

Later pyramids were built with smooth, slanted sides. They represented the Benben or sacred mound upon which the sun god stood to create the universe.

Perhaps the most famous of all pyramids is the Great Pyramid of King Khufu at Giza. It is vast. Over 2,300,000 separate blocks of limestone, some weighing as much as 33,000

pounds, were dragged into position to construct it. The pyramid covers 275 square yards and, originally, stood 479 feet high.

The Great Pyramid was built by a work force of over 5,000 workers who spent every day for twenty years on the pyramid site. They included skilled craftsmen, quarry workers, and general workers who cut up the limestone blocks, pulled them along mud ramps into place, and then covered the pyramid with a layer of gleaming limestone.

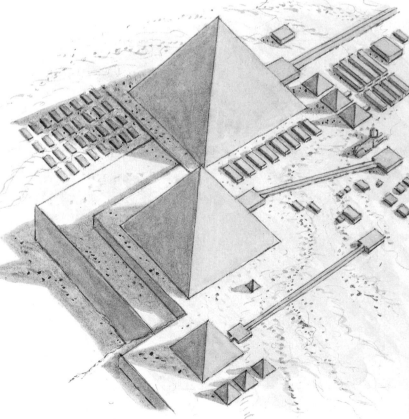

The pyramids of Giza

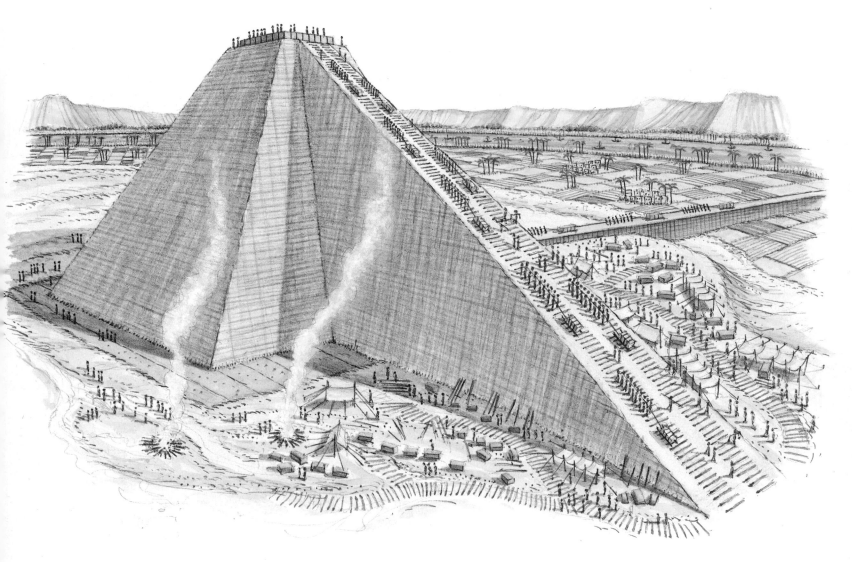

Workers drag stones up a mud ramp to build a pyramid.

In addition to these workers, agricultural workers helped out for three or four months every year when the Nile flooded the fields.

Later, the Pharaohs were buried in rock tombs cut into the limestone cliffs at Thebes. This area is called the Valley of the Kings. Tutankhamun's tomb is here. It is a small tomb and not at all typical of royal tombs in the valley. It was probably originally intended for one of his high officials.

Many treasures and large quantities of gold were buried with a Pharaoh. Therefore, architects tried to make the tombs safe from tomb robbers. In addition to stealing the treasures, the robbers would hack at the king's body to steal any jewelry in the mummy wrappings. Sometimes they set fire to the gold coffins to melt off the metal. To prevent such destruction, huge granite plugs or gates were fixed in the corridors of the pyramids.

In the Valley of the Kings, a well, or shaft, was often sunk in the main corridor of the tomb. In addition, a false wall was built on the other side of the shaft to make it look as if the tomb had come to an end.

Thieves still managed to get into the tombs, and occasionally they were caught. Then they were put on trial and forced to confess how they got into the tomb. The culprits were brutally executed by being thrust upon the points of sharp stakes stuck into the ground and left to die in agony. But the tomb thieves of Ancient Egypt were not put off by this punishment. All the royal tombs, except those of Tutankhamun at Thebes and Psusennes at Tanis, were robbed.

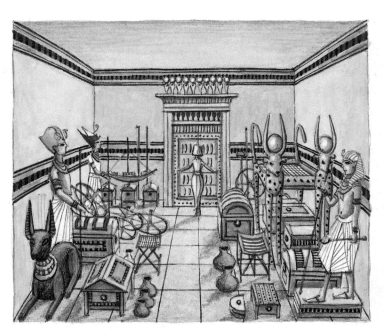

"The glitter of gold" — some of the equipment for a royal tomb

RELIGION

Obelisk barge being towed to the temple

Celebrations at a temple festival

Rock-cut temple

Terraced temple

Priests and Pharaoh worshiping the sun god

Temple craftsman making an incense burner

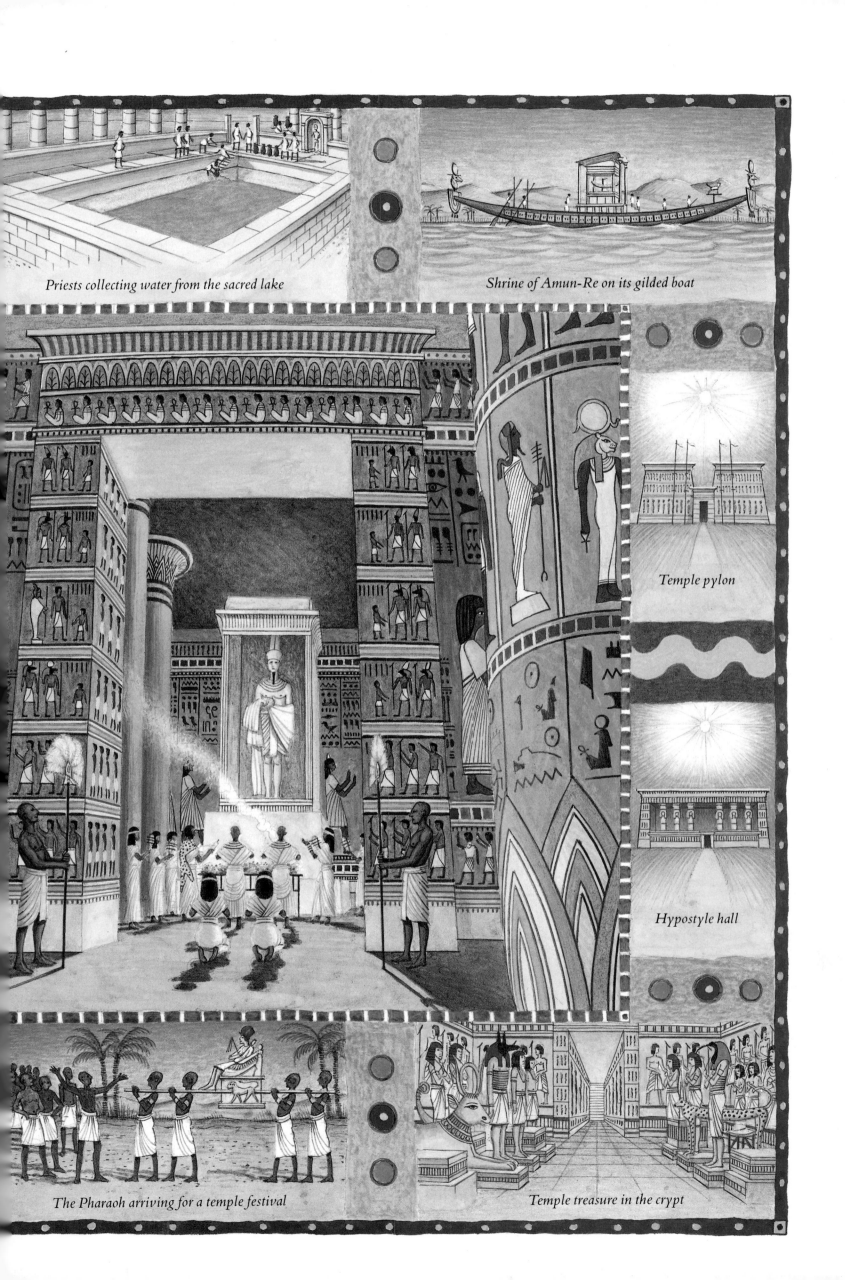

Priests collecting water from the sacred lake

Shrine of Amun-Re on its gilded boat

Temple pylon

Hypostyle hall

The Pharaoh arriving for a temple festival

Temple treasure in the crypt

GODS AND GODDESSES

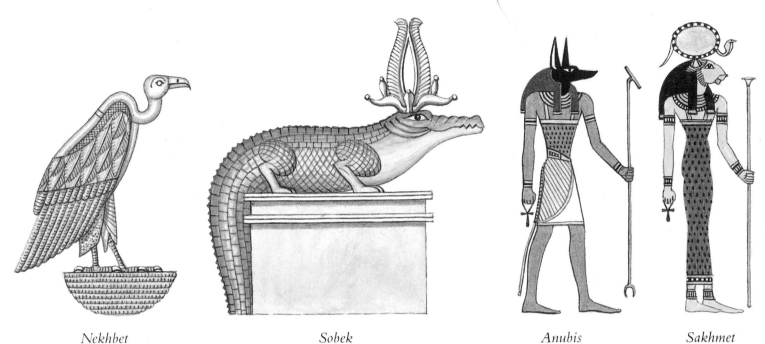

Nekhbet   *Sobek*   *Anubis*   *Sakhmet*

The names of hundreds of gods and goddesses survive from Ancient Egypt. Many were worshiped in temples while others belonged to the Underworld.

The Egyptians believed that gods and goddesses could take on the forms of particular birds or animals. For example, Nekhbet was the vulture goddess and Sobek was the crocodile god. The Egyptians also believed that a god could take on a human form. Many pictures and statues show gods as part creature, part human. For example, Anubis had a jackal's head on a male body; Sakhmet had a lioness's head on a female body.

Not every animal of a species by which a god could reveal himself was considered holy. For instance, there was only one kind of bull that was sacred to the god Ptah of Memphis. It was called Apis, and its hide had to be black with a white triangular patch of hair between the horns. Like the Pharaoh, it lived in a palace and took part in state ceremonies. When it died, it was mummified, decked out with jewelry, and buried in a huge granite coffin. Many generations of these Apis bulls were buried in a huge underground gallery at Saqqara. It is called the Serapeum.

Ptah   *Apis*   *Apophis*   *Thoth*

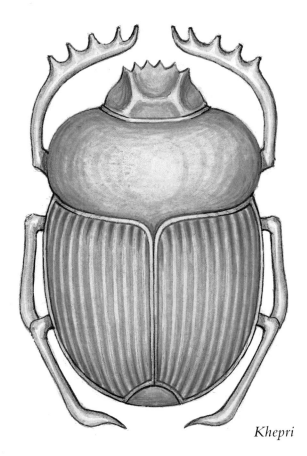

Khepri

Re-Horakhty

Of all the gods and goddesses, the sun god was the most important. The Egyptians were always glad when he rose above the hills of the eastern desert at dawn. At night, when he sank into the western horizon, the Egyptians imagined that the evil snake, Apophis, would try to swallow the sun god as he passed through the Underworld.

The sun god was portrayed in different ways with different names. As the scarab beetle he was Khepri or "He Who Comes Into Being." With this image, the Sun was symbolized as the creator god. Real scarab beetles push balls of dirt along the ground, and the Egyptians imagined that the Sun might be pushed through the sky in the same way. Young scarabs appear to be born from the ball of dirt because the female scarab lays her eggs inside the ball, where they hatch. This image symbolized the sun god at the beginning of time coming out of the water to create the universe.

The sun god was also called Atum, meaning "totality," and Re, which referred to the fiery Sun itself. In this form he could join with the god Horus. He was then called Re-Horakhty, which means "Re as Horus of the Horizon." He was shown as a hawk with the Sun on its head encircled by the cobra goddess. During Egypt's greatest time, the sun became combined with Amun, the god of Thebes. He was then known as Amun-Re, king of the gods.

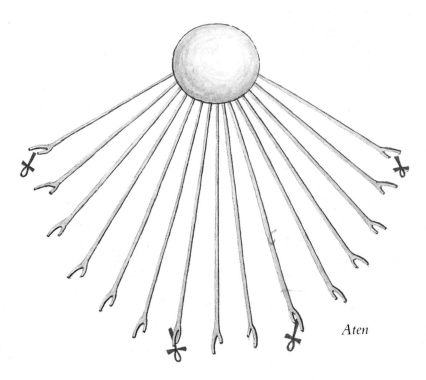

Aten

The Pharaoh, Akhenaten, had his own ideas about the sun god. He had it shown as a disk with rays ending as hands. This form was called Aten.

MYTHOLOGY

There are many legends from ancient Egyptian belief. Some of the most interesting legends are about how the universe came into existence. One story says that in the very beginning of time the only thing that existed was water, called Nun. A mound, or Benben, arose from it, and on this Re, the sun god, stood. The Egyptians got this idea from the mud hillocks that gradually appeared each year out of the river Nile as the floodwaters went down. Re created air and moisture by spitting and as a result the god Shu and the goddess Tefnut came into being. Tefnut gave birth to the earth god, Geb, and the sky goddess, Nut.

The Egyptians also had ideas about how the human race was created. Humans were made either from the tears of the sun god or out of clay by the ram-headed god Khnum.

Another myth tells how mankind was nearly wiped out. The sun god Re once became annoyed, believing that man was plotting against him. One morning he sent his "eye" down to Egypt to punish them. This eye took on the form of the lioness Sakhmet, who killed people so eagerly that, by evening, almost all the Egyptians were destroyed. While Sakhmet slept, Re held a council of gods and told them

Heh, god of infinity; Geb, the earth god (lying down); and the goddess Hathor, daughter of Re

that things had gone too far. If all men were killed, no one would look after the gods' temples or leave offerings on festival days. So, that night, the gods went down to Egypt and covered the whole land with beer that was stained red with ocher. The next day, the goddess Sakhmet returned to continue the killing and saw the country covered in what she thought was blood. She drank it and became drunk, fell asleep, and forgot about destroying mankind.

Another legend, about Osiris, was also important to the Egyptians.

In a golden age, Osiris ruled Egypt as god-king with his queen, the goddess Isis. Seth, Osiris's wicked brother, was jealous, and he plotted to get the throne for himself. At a

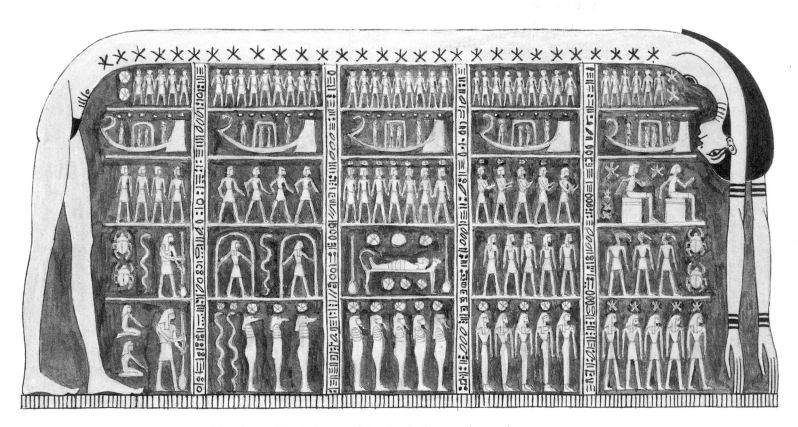

An ancient Egyptian impression of the sky goddess Nut stretching her body over the earth

Above: *Horus in the double crown spears his enemy Seth, who attacks in the form of a hippopotamus.*

Below: *The temple of Isis and (inset) the god Osiris, king of the Underworld*

banquet he offered a very valuable chest to whoever could fit inside it. It had been carefully made to fit Osiris. When Osiris climbed into it, Seth slammed the lid shut and threw it into the Nile. Isis and her sister, Nephthys, searched for the chest and discovered, at last, that when it had been washed ashore, a tree had grown up around it. The tree had been cut down and used, with the chest still inside, as a column in the royal palace. Isis returned to the palace and demanded that she be given the tree with the body of Osiris in it. She hid the body in the marshes, but one day Seth discovered it. He cut it into pieces and scattered the bits throughout Egypt. Isis and Nephthys gathered all the parts together, and Isis managed to bring Osiris back to life. Isis had Osiris's child, Horus, and Osiris became ruler of the Underworld.

When Horus grew up, he struggled with Seth for many years to gain control of the throne of Egypt. Eventually, a tribunal of gods was established to decide who should rule Egypt. Finally, Isis tricked Seth into admitting his guilt, and Horus was given the throne of Egypt.

PRIESTS AND TEMPLE RITUAL

Priests looked after the temples and estates of the gods and goddesses. Some temples were quite small with perhaps just a columned kiosk for the statue. Others, such as the temple of Amun at Thebes, were surrounded by huge areas of land and brought in much money. The high priest had great power, and he looked after the money received from the temple lands.

Priestesses were also powerful, particularly the high priestess of Amun who was thought of as the bride of the king of the gods. Priestesses often provided ritual music by shaking their sacred rattles, called sistra, or their necklaces, which were thick with beads.

Ordinary priests were given titles such as Pure Ones or Divine Fathers. It was their job to sweep away dust and sand and organize the offerings needed in the rituals. In many temples priests had to shave all the hair from their heads and bodies as a sign of ritual cleanliness. The god of the temple would be angry if creatures such as lice were accidentally brought into his temple in the hair of a priest. For the same reason, no animal skins could be used for clothes, although one kind of priest could wear a panther skin over his linen robes. Some of the

Priestesses shake their sacred rattles.

priests washed themselves in the pure water of the sacred lake within the temple grounds.

The priests had a list of their duties, and for every single hour of the day at least one priest would be on duty in the temple. Some priests would have been given special jobs, such as reading, singing the hymns during ceremonies, or roasting incense for the rituals in front of the statues of the god.

Incense is burned for the crucial rituals in the temple sanctuary while priests perform their special duties.

The high priest dedicates lavish food offerings to the cult statue of the god Amun.

The golden statue of the chief god or goddess was kept locked in a shrine. Only the highest members of the priesthood were allowed to open it. The golden shrine could be taken out of its granite sanctuary for festival celebrations. Priests carried it around the temple on their shoulders on a wooden boat about ten feet long.

Every morning, the high priest approached the shrine saying the words, "I am a Pure One." The high priest drew back the bolt on the shrine doors and broke the clay seal. Fresh linen robes and fine gold jewelry, such as necklaces and pendants, were put on the statue. The priest then offered food for the god's breakfast and left the sanctuary. Of course, the food would still be on the offering table when the high priest returned. It was thought that the god or goddess either was dining elsewhere or that he or she had eaten the "spirit" of the food. The priests were then allowed to eat the food themselves. At night, the shrine was sealed and bolted until the next morning when the high priest began the ritual again.

POPULAR RELIGION AND MAGIC

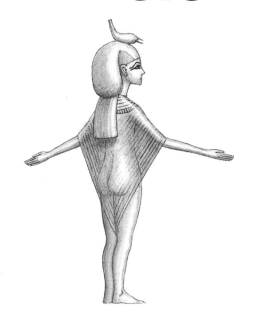

Serket Re

Taweret

Most Egyptians were not allowed into the temples because they were considered to be unpure. Although many farmers worked on temple estates and lots of craftsmen made furniture and jewelry for use in the temples, they were not included in the secret rituals. Only during religious festivals could ordinary people catch a glimpse of the shrine hiding a divine statue as it was carried from one temple to another. In fact, major gods and goddesses with magnificent temples were not important in the daily lives of ordinary Egyptians.

Many Egyptians worshiped particular gods and goddesses that helped with everyday problems at home and at work. One very anxious time for a family was when a woman was about to have a baby. Two goddesses were supposed to protect her: Meskhenet and Taweret (Great One). Taweret looked very ferocious. She had the head of a snarling hippopotamus, the limbs of a lioness, and a large belly. She stopped evil creatures from attacking the woman or child. A woman who was expecting a baby wore charms shaped like Taweret on necklaces or bracelets.

Another god who protected newly-born babies was Bes. He was a fat dwarf with the ears and mane of a lion and was shown poking out his tongue.

Bes

Meretseger

Isis

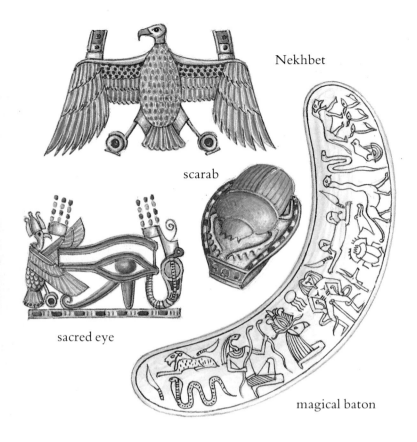

Nekhbet

scarab

sacred eye

magical baton

Jewelry and amulets were supposed to give the wearer protection. Pictured on the magical baton are gods and goddesses who warded off dangers in the house.

If a child became ill, the goddess Isis was called upon to come and cool the burning fever with her saliva.

Snakes and scorpions were a real hazard in Ancient Egypt. The workmen who cut out the tombs in the Valley of the Kings prayed to the cobra goddess Meretseger if they were bitten or stung. People used magic wands made of ivory and shaped like boomerangs to draw a circle around their sleeping quarters to prevent snakes and scorpions from entering.

Small stone objects shaped like a shield were carved with scenes showing the dangers of life in the Nile Valley and held the magical means to avoid them. They showed the young god Horus in the center. He stood on the backs of crocodiles to stop any real crocodiles from catching and eating the family. In his hands, he held snakes, scorpions, and lions to keep them away from the family. Spells were carved in the stone to give it even greater magical power.

Spells were often used to cure illnesses and even to act as lovecharms.

The god Horus, as a child, keeps dangerous creatures such as snakes, scorpions, and crocodiles away from the family.

SCRIBES AND CRAFTSMEN

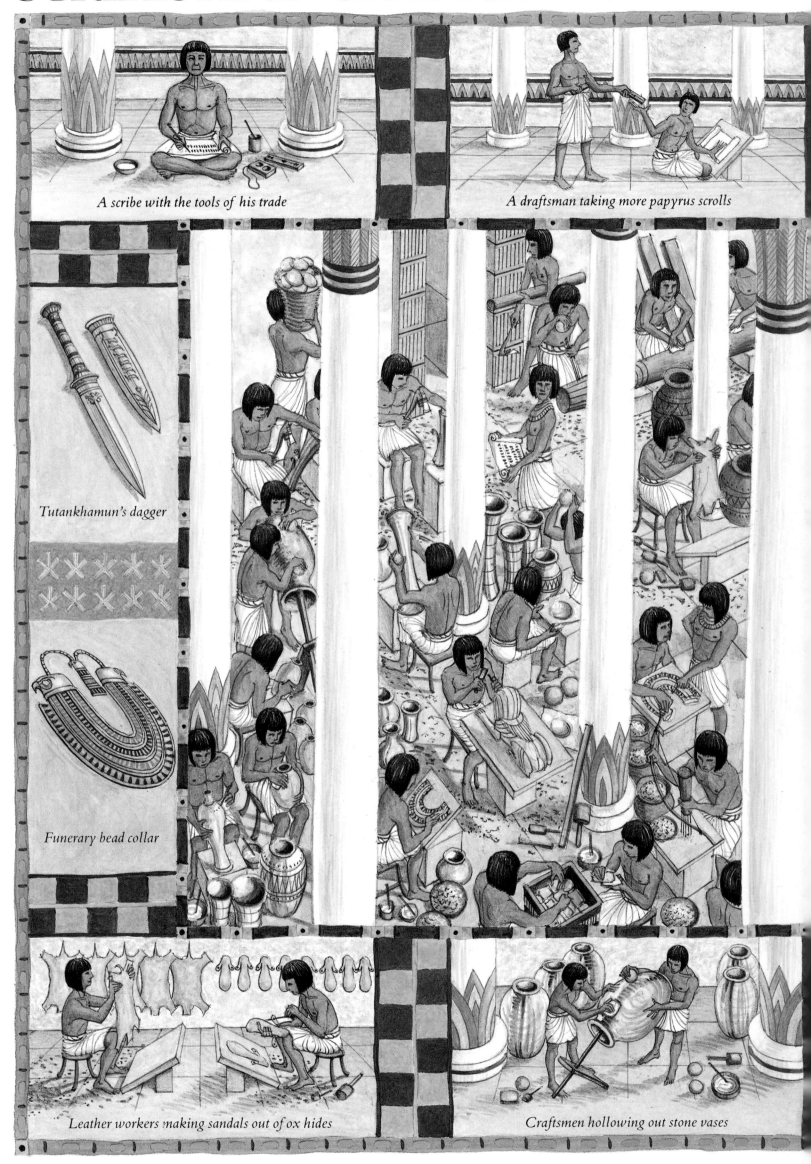

A scribe with the tools of his trade

A draftsman taking more papyrus scrolls

Tutankhamun's dagger

Funerary bead collar

Leather workers making sandals out of ox hides

Craftsmen hollowing out stone vases

A scribe making a dedication to his patron god Thoth

A scribe at work counting cattle

Scarab pectoral

Finger rings

Carpenters using a bow drill while making a bed

A jeweler polishing stones

EDUCATION AND HIEROGLYPHS

All great state officials were trained scribes. Scribes in Ancient Egypt were highly privileged. A scribe was called "everybody's boss," and training to become one was hard work.

Young scribes were sent to learn their skills in a place known as the House of Life. Normally, only the sons of scribes were trained to write. They served an apprenticeship to senior scribes, probably for about four to five years. Much of their time was spent copying texts of letters, accounts, and adventure stories. They practiced on sheets of papyrus or less expensive wooden boards coated with plaster and limestone flakes.

You can imagine that many young scribes were jealous when they saw the sons of craftsmen and farmers playing games outside. But the tutors reminded them that after all their studies were over, they would be in a much better position than their friends.

While in the House of Life, the pupils could look at documents that might help them in their future jobs. One scribe might practice writing out the names of foreign towns.

Another might concentrate on problems such as the division of bread or beer among workers.

The scribes did not have to work on building sites or irrigation canals as everyone else did. Instead they drew up the lists of people to do this work. Scribes also collected taxes for the king, landowners, or temples. A scribe might leave the House of Life and work on a nobleman's estate, recording the number of geese or cattle for a tax count. If he kept the records in good order, he could be promoted to inspector of accountant scribes. He might be recommended for a job in the royal household as a king's scribe. The most desirable job was vizier or prime minister.

The Ancient Egyptians used two scripts to write their language. The earliest script was the picture writing that we call hieroglyphs, a Greek word meaning "sacred carvings." This script was in use for over 3,000 years on state monuments, temples, and tombs. There were about 700 different signs that the scribes had to learn.

Pupils in the House of Life learn to be scribes. Some pupils could not help wishing they were playing with their friends.

An example of hieroglyphs concerning Nefertari, with a translation

Sign	Pronounced		Sign	Pronounced
cobra	djed		vulture	mut
walking stick	medu		loaf of bread	t
flowering reed	i		heart and windpipe	nefer
water	n		flowering reed	i
eye			loaf of bread	t
	wesir		mouth	r
throne			two strokes	y
seated god	not pronounced		water	n
sedge plant	nesu		irrigation channel	mer
well	hem		loaf of bread	t
loaf of bread	t		plinth (statue base)	maa
swallow	wes		oar	kheru
mouth	r			
loaf of bread	t			

The first column of hieroglyphs would be pronounced:
djed medu in Wesir hemet nesu weret
and translated as:
spoken words by Osiris wife of the king great

The second column of hieroglyphs would be pronounced:
Neferitery meret n Mut
and translated as:
Nefertari beloved of Mut

The meaning of these hieroglyphs is therefore: Words spoken by the Osirified (i.e., dead and treated as a goddess) Great Royal Wife Nefertari, beloved of Mut (wife of Amun Re, king of the gods).

PAPYRUSES

Scribes wrote on papyrus scrolls. They were made from freshly gathered papyrus reeds that grew along the Nile, especially in the delta. The reeds were cut about twelve inches above the river level. The outer rind was peeled away and the stem was cut into strips. These strips were placed on the ground and overlaid with more strips arranged crosswise. The strips were then covered with a linen cloth and pounded vigorously so that they joined together in their own sap to make a sheet. A series of sheets would then be joined together with gum to make a papyrus scroll.

Scribes wrote on papyrus with fine brushes made of plant fiber. Usually they wrote in black ink made from soot and water, but important headings were written in red ink made from desert ocher. When scribes wrote, they sat cross-legged and stretched their linen kilts across their knees as tightly as possible to create a hard enough surface to write on. They used their kilts as desktops and rested their scrolls on them.

1. *Papyrus reeds are gathered from the marshes.*

2. *The lower stems are cut up into strips.*

3. *The strips are pounded into a sheet.*

4. *The sheets are joined with gum to make a scroll.*

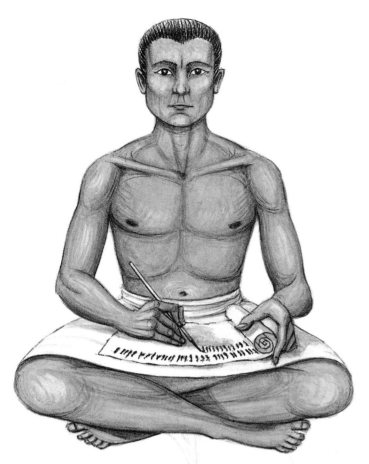

A scribe with his reed pen and papyrus

more serious. One sort is all about good behavior and is often called "wisdom literature." These papyruses usually consist of a set of instructions from an elderly scribe, often to his son. They contain advice on how to deal with quarrelsome, hot-tempered, and greedy people. They urge a scribe to keep calm in a crisis, to aspire to be a "truly quiet man."

Scientific papyruses have been found that give information on medicine, surgery, mathematics, and astronomy. The medical papyruses tell us that the Egyptians thought the heart had vital control throughout the body and that it "spoke" through the pulse. They gave advice to doctors on how to treat burns, tumors, eye diseases, and stomach ailments. Mathematical papyruses are full of problems for scribes to study that involve everyday situations. They show examples of how to divide rations among workmen, how to calculate the area of fields, or how to arrive at the area of a circle. Astronomical papyruses had information about the movement of the stars.

Because the climate of Egypt is so dry, thousands of papyrus fragments and some complete scrolls have survived. They cover a variety of subjects. Some are stories, like the tales of enchantment in the Arabian *A Thousand and One Nights*. Others are far

The Egyptians also had a simple form of what we call psychology in their interpretation of dreams. For example, if a man saw a large cat in a dream, it was a good sign because it meant there would be a very good harvest.

A scribe's sense of humor is shown on this papyrus cartoon of animals pretending to be people.

CRAFTSMEN AND ARTISTS

Craftsmen worked for the Pharaoh, his officials, and the priests. They included potters, carpenters, stonemasons, jewelry-makers, metalworkers, bronzesmiths, and artists.

Early pots were made by hand using coils of clay. Some were a buff color with red designs of boats and ostriches. Others were red with black insides and outer rims. The black color was created by placing the pots upside down in smoldering ashes. Later a circular platform was developed that could be spun by the hand or the feet. This was the potter's wheel.

Carpenters were needed for a variety of tasks. They made boats, furniture, coffins, and huge doors for palaces and temples.

Stonemasons had to be able to cut the hardest stones with the simplest tools. Granite from the quarries at Aswan was the most difficult stone of all to work with. It was used for temple obelisks that could weigh over 550 tons.

Other kinds of stone were easier to carve. Sandstone was used to build temples, and limestone was the material used for most statues.

Stonemasons at work in a granite quarry

Workers on scaffolding carve the sphinx.

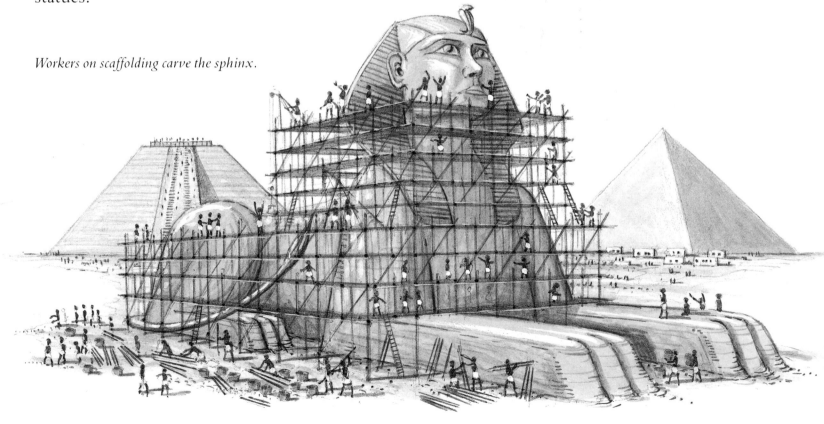

32

Much of Egyptian jewelry glitters with gold because there was an almost endless supply from the mines in the eastern deserts. The deserts also supplied the jeweler with semiprecious stones for bracelets and necklaces. Among these stones were orange-colored carnelian, green feldspar, mauve amethyst, and turquoise. The most highly prized stone of all — deep-blue lapis lazuli — had to be imported from as far away as Afghanistan. To heat metal, the jewelers blew down pipes into a furnace to raise the temperature. A better method was a foot-bellows, which created much higher temperatures.

Bronzesmiths made many statuettes of gods and goddesses that officials could then dedicate and place in temples. First they made a model in beeswax and coated it with clay, leaving a small hole in the base. The whole thing was then heated so that the clay hardened and the wax could be poured out through the hole. The clay kept the shape of the model, and the bronzesmiths then poured molten bronze through the hole. When it cooled, the mold was broken off to reveal the bronze model.

Artists were always needed. They decorated tomb and temple walls with colors that were easy to find. These were mainly blues and greens from ground-up minerals such as azurite and malachite, reds and yellows from desert ochers, white from limestone, and black from soot. Brightly colored scenes of, for example, wildlife in the marshes still astound us today with their detail and freshness. It is difficult to believe that in many cases the craftsmen worked deep in a tomb with only the artificial light of bronze reflectors or lamps.

A painter puts the final brush strokes on an elaborately painted royal tomb, aided by a reflector.

LIFE IN THE HOME

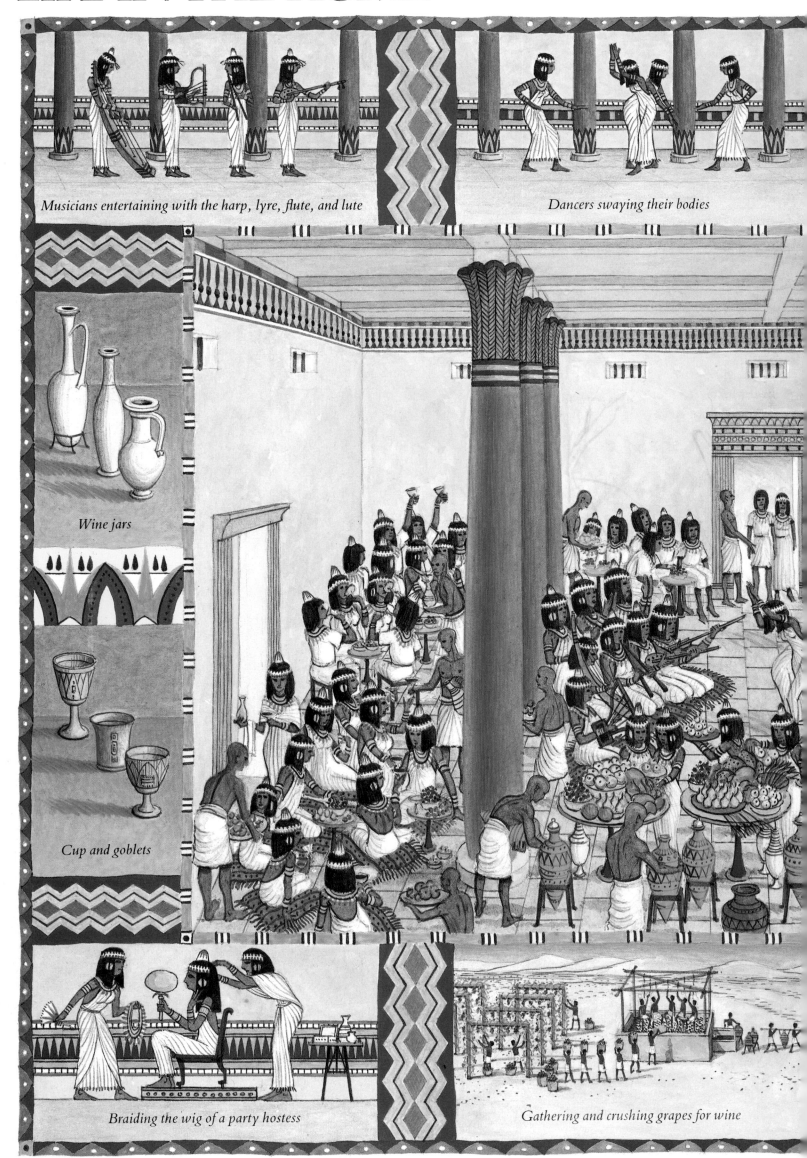

Musicians entertaining with the harp, lyre, flute, and lute

Dancers swaying their bodies

Wine jars

Cup and goblets

Braiding the wig of a party hostess

Gathering and crushing grapes for wine

Maidservants looking after party guests

Singers performing a popular song

Figs and grapes

Pomegranates and dates

Servants preparing a course of roast duck

Presenting guests with flowers at a party

HOUSES AND FURNITURE

Only a few towns of Ancient Egypt survive today. There are several reasons. Buildings were made of mud brick, a material that, if neglected, easily crumbles. Egyptian farmers carried off tons of mud bricks to use as a sort of fertilizer on their crops. Many small towns have disappeared below the silt of the Nile floodplain, and others lie below modern cities such as Cairo and Alexandria.

The foundations of some important towns have survived, though. One set of foundations was from a town for workmen, priests, and officials connected with a pyramid site known today as Illahun. Another is the remains of el-Amarna, the short-lived capital of Egypt during the reign of Akhenaten. The village of the workers on the royal tombs, in the Valley of the Kings, was discovered at the site known as Deir el-Medina.

From studying the ruins and pictures on papyruses, we have a good idea of what the buildings in which the ancient Egyptians lived were like. The bricks for houses were made from the Nile silt. Bits of stone and chaff were mixed with the mud to help the bricks bind together. They were shaped in wooden frames and then dried in the sun.

The Egyptians loved color. The walls of a nobleman's villa were coated with limestone plaster and then painted with scenes, perhaps of calves leaping in the fields or pintail ducks flying up from clumps of papyrus. There were a few windows with grills across them. They were high up in the wall to prevent too much direct sunlight and dust from getting indoors. The main reception room might have had stone bases for wooden columns that helped to support a ceiling of palm logs. Bedrooms, bathroom cubicles, and a kitchen led off from this central hall. In the evening, the family could go up onto the roof, where there were small pavilions to sit in. They caught the cool breeze blowing from the north, which was a welcome relief from the hot sun of the day.

Ordinary houses might have had one large room and a courtyard for animals and storage. These houses also had facilities on the roof for the family to relax in.

Many pieces of ancient furniture have survived. Gilded chests for jewels or clothes were protected by charms of Isis and Osiris carved on them. Some chairs had legs in the shape of lions' paws and were inlaid with ivory and ebony.

A spacious villa of a nobleman, showing living rooms, storage areas, granary, and cattle pen

One strange feature of Egyptian furniture was the headrest. This was a low, horseshoe-shaped frame secured to a wooden base with a pillow placed in its curve. The design of the headrest would allow air to circulate. It also kept venemous scorpions or snakes away from the head of a person sleeping on, or close to, the ground.

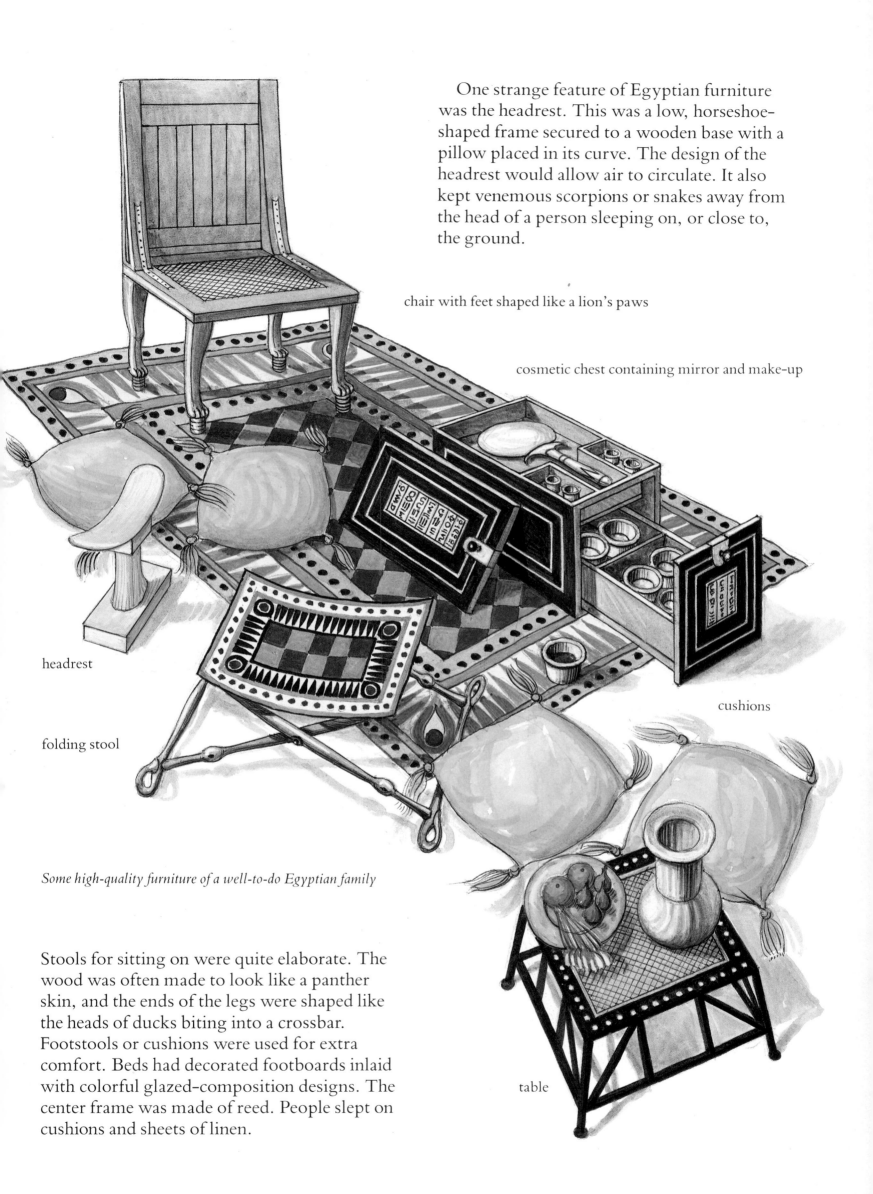

chair with feet shaped like a lion's paws

cosmetic chest containing mirror and make-up

headrest

cushions

folding stool

Some high-quality furniture of a well-to-do Egyptian family

Stools for sitting on were quite elaborate. The wood was often made to look like a panther skin, and the ends of the legs were shaped like the heads of ducks biting into a crossbar. Footstools or cushions were used for extra comfort. Beds had decorated footboards inlaid with colorful glazed-composition designs. The center frame was made of reed. People slept on cushions and sheets of linen.

table

WOMEN AND ADORNMENT

Women in Ancient Egypt had a more liberated position than women in many countries of the ancient world. They could practice professions and have property in their own names. In fact, there were laws that protected women and their property.

Very few women learned to write the hieroglyphs that took scribes such a long time to master, but they were trained in other skills.

Most women thought of marriage as the first major event in their lives. Most marriages were an alliance of property between families, with the bride retaining full rights over the goods or land she brought with her. Upon marriage, a woman usually took the title of Lady of the House. She then supervised all the servants and nursemaids.

Pictures and the remains of linen garments and wigs show us much about women's fashions in Ancient Egypt. Dresses were made of linen that varied in quality. They had many pleats and were usually white or dyed orange, yellow, or green. Straps of linen supported the dress unless it was woven as a complete garment. Some pictures show servant girls wearing beaded nets over their dresses. This was not only for decoration. The beads prevented the linen from being rubbed and frayed.

Household servants carry fruit and wine to the dinner table while a woman plays the harp and a cat waits hopefully for scraps.

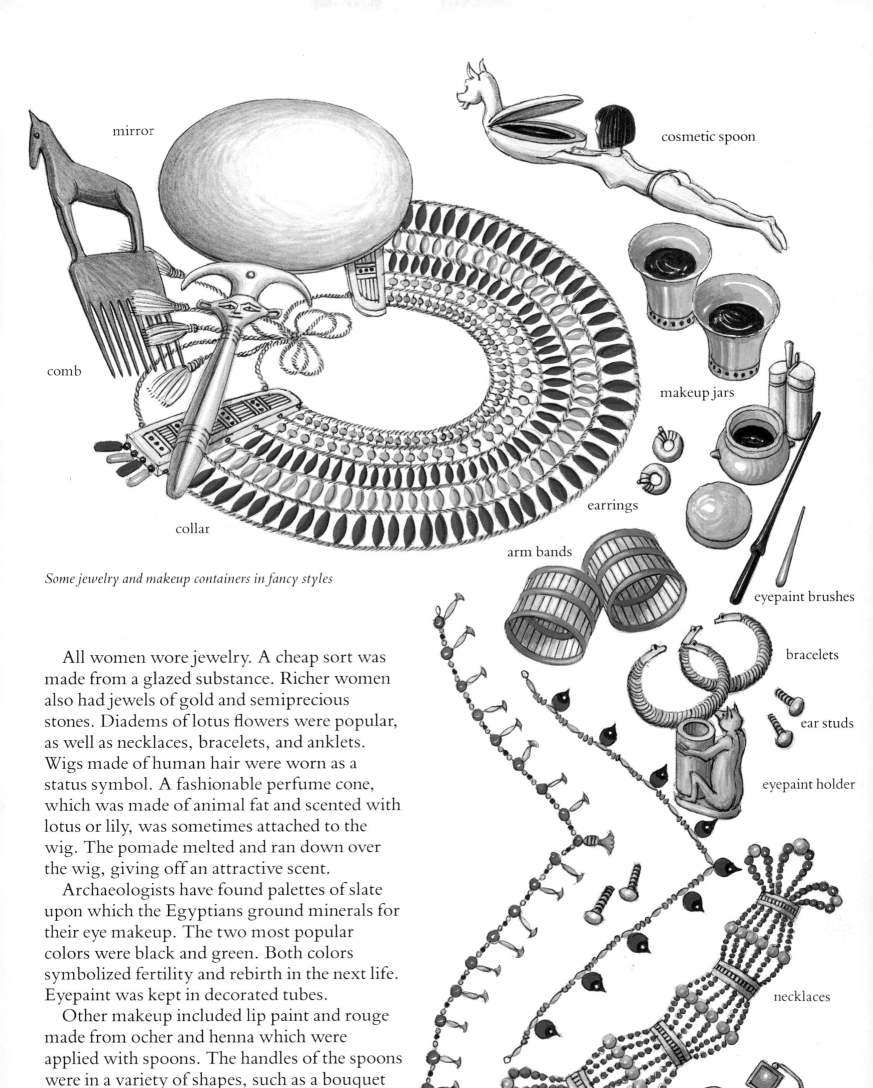

mirror

cosmetic spoon

comb

makeup jars

collar

earrings

arm bands

eyepaint brushes

bracelets

ear studs

eyepaint holder

necklaces

rings

Some jewelry and makeup containers in fancy styles

All women wore jewelry. A cheap sort was made from a glazed substance. Richer women also had jewels of gold and semiprecious stones. Diadems of lotus flowers were popular, as well as necklaces, bracelets, and anklets. Wigs made of human hair were worn as a status symbol. A fashionable perfume cone, which was made of animal fat and scented with lotus or lily, was sometimes attached to the wig. The pomade melted and ran down over the wig, giving off an attractive scent.

Archaeologists have found palettes of slate upon which the Egyptians ground minerals for their eye makeup. The two most popular colors were black and green. Both colors symbolized fertility and rebirth in the next life. Eyepaint was kept in decorated tubes.

Other makeup included lip paint and rouge made from ocher and henna which were applied with spoons. The handles of the spoons were in a variety of shapes, such as a bouquet of flowers, a jackal biting the tail of a fish, or a duck with its head twisted back to feed the ducklings traveling on its back.

CHILDREN

On the estate of a high court official in Ancient Egypt, you would have found lots of children playing games. Some of the games, such as tug-of-war, are familiar to us today.

Children of modern Egypt still play the game of *khazza lawizza*. It is a sort of leapfrog where two children sit facing each other on the ground with their legs stretched out and their hands touching. Other children then have to jump over them as their arms are gradually raised higher. On tomb walls, there are pictures that were carved over 4,500 years ago of children playing this game.

Some boys pretended they were soldiers capturing an enemy. Another game was based on putting up trellises for vines. Boys balanced on one another to form a human vine trellis. Girls played different games. They are often shown spinning around in a circle supported by other girls in the center.

Dancing was very popular. In one dance the girls held mirrors, kicked their legs high, and swung their hair, which had been braided and tied with a clay ball. This vigorous dance was in honor of Hathor, the goddess of joy.

Below: *Children play games outdoors, including forms of leapfrog and ball catching, as well as throwing sticks for games of chance.*

leopard with movable lower jaw

horse on wheels

"paddle" doll

knuckle bones

Above and opposite: *A selection of toys*

Both children and their parents enjoyed playing board games. One very ancient game was called Serpent. A round stone was carved to look like a coiled snake with its body divided into segments. Moving a counter according to the fall of bones or sticks, each player tried to be first to reach the snake's head in the center.

A game called Senet was also popular. In this game, a rectangular board was divided into three lines of squares. Each of two players had counters, either conical or barrel-shaped. The aim was to go along each of the two outer lines and to be the first to reach the end of the center line, moving the counter after each throw. Some squares had symbols on them. If players landed on a symbol that meant beauty or power, they would then have an advantage added to their turn. But if they landed on a bad-luck sign, such as rough water, they had to pay a penalty.

Among the toys we know that Egyptian children played with were little wooden dolls with hair made out of small beads of mud. Models of monkeys on horseback also used to amuse children. Evidence of toys that moved has been found, including a horse on wheels, a mouse with a movable mouth and tail, and a wooden cat with a jaw that was operated by pulling a papyrus twine attached to it.

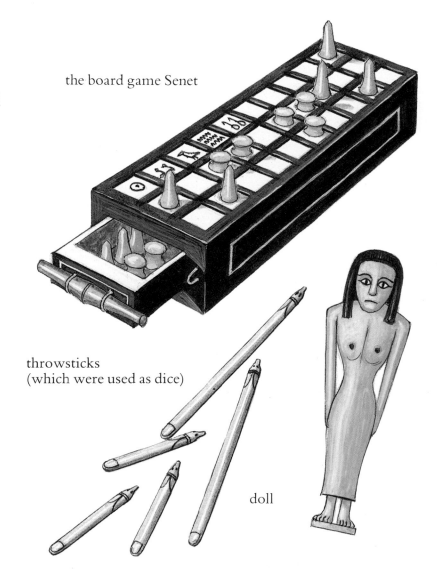

the board game Senet

throwsticks
(which were used as dice)

doll

41

THE FAMILY AT LEISURE

A nobleman and his family picnic in the garden while fan bearers keep everyone cool.

The garden was one place where parents and children could relax together. Shade was provided by sycamore-fig trees, date palms, and acacia trees. Some families had an ornamental pool in their garden, which was filled with Nile water conducted through a small canal. There were probably ducks, fish, and lilies in it. It would have had a small border of silt for shrubs and plants and have been surrounded by a path. The family sat here under the trees or perhaps in a pavilion at the end of the pool.

Families also went bird hunting together on the papyrus marshes. Paintings show that the whole family enjoyed the hunt. They sailed through the thickets on skiffs made from papyrus. The father stood at the prow of the boat and sometimes tried to hide from the birds by holding some herons out in front of him. In his hand he held a throw-stick. It was sometimes shaped like a snake so that it could magically "bite" into the birds. Other sticks looked a bit like boomerangs. When he was close to a bird, the father would throw the stick to stun it.

A nobleman and his wife relax under a canopy as they sail north on the Nile. Rowers propel the boat while a man at the stern steers it.
Inset: *A cat with birds (taken from a painting in the tomb of the courtier Nebaum)*

We know that some people took the family cat hunting with them. The cat ran along the edge of the marsh to scare the birds into flight. Then the hunter could get a better shot at the birds. In the tomb of a courtier called Nebaum, a painting shows his cat balancing on papyrus stalks, with a duck between its teeth and two birds in its claws which were a reward for its work.

People also went fishing with spears, but the most dangerous sport on the river was hunting hippopotamuses. They were killed because they were dangerous to small boats and often trampled crops close to the river.

In the evening, the family might have had a party. The guests were given flowers to hold and floral necklaces. There might have been bread, cakes, figs, grapes, ducks, and beef to eat, and wine to drink. The guests were entertained by dancing girls and female musicians who played the harp, lute, and flute. Although we know what the instruments would have sounded like, no written music from Ancient Egypt has yet been found.

EGYPTIANS AT WORK

A farmer operating a water sweep (shaduf)

Girls squabbling over ears of barley

Plows

Sickle and winnowing trays

A tax agent inspecting a boundary stone

Geese being rounded up and counted

A nursing mother helping in the fields, preparing food

A thirsty field worker drinking from a waterskin

The granary

Mattock and hoes

Men competing with sacred baboons to gather figs

Donkeys carrying barley to the granary

WORK IN THE FIELDS

Scribes make a note of the level of the Nile in a Nilometer to see whether to expect a low or high flood.

The farmer's year was centered around what happened to the Nile. Toward the end of July, the star Sirius could be seen at dawn above the horizon. Such an occurrence indicated that the annual Nile flood was about to happen. The river flooded the land right up to the edge of the deserts. In November, the water subsided, leaving behind a rich silt. Today, the high dam at Aswan keeps the river at a set height.

The Egyptian year consisted of three seasons of four months. Every month had thirty days making a year 360 days long. The Egyptians then added five days as gods' birthdays. They did not add the day we add on each leap year, so after a while their festivals began to fall in the wrong month. They therefore adjusted the calendar to make it right again!

The new year began with the rising of the Nile water. There were two problems that might occur in the flood season. The flood could be very high, and villages normally on safe ground might be swept away. Or the flood might be low, which meant that it did not cover enough land with fertile silt. If the flood was low for several years, then famine was likely. Nilometers, which consisted of notches on walls marking previous flood levels, were used to measure the flood. Priests read the level at the beginning of the year and compared it with an average year to see if it was higher or lower. The people in charge of the land then knew what to expect.

The sowing season began when the Nile flood had subsided. If the ground began to harden, men used mattocks to break it up. Then a farmer scattered barley or emmer wheat over the field. He was followed by two cattle drawing a plow. Finally, a herd of goats or a flock of sheep were driven over the field so that their hooves could firmly embed the seed into the ground.

The fields were kept watered by canals fed with water from the Nile. Water was raised over the bank to the higher level of the canal by *shadufs*. These were poles on pivots with a clay weight on one end that balanced a bucket at the other.

The summer season was harvest time. The ripe crop was cut by reapers using curved wooden sickles with flint teeth. All members of the farmer's family helped. Women and children gathered up wisps of wheat. There exists a picture that shows two girls fighting over the same ear of wheat!

The crop was then taken to the threshing floor, where oxen trod away the stalks before the workers winnowed it between wooden trays. The people wore linen scarves around their heads to protect their hair as they threw up the wheat and chaff, allowing the lighter chaff to blow away. Donkeys then took the grain to the granaries.

Men sow the seed, which is plowed into the silt and trodden down firmly by sheep and goats. Fields are kept watered by a shaduf.

FOOD AND DRINK

Granaries were very important to the ancient Egyptians. They contained the grain that could be used in time of famine. They were protected by high walls and overseers. Every sack of grain that was taken out was recorded by a scribe.

Bread was the staple diet of the Egyptians. Bakers made a very coarse bread from barley. The grain was ground on a stone, mixed with water, and then rolled into dough. It was baked in a beehive-shaped oven. Bits of stone from the grinding or grit from the desert could get into the bread. Recent studies of mummies show that the teeth of many Egyptians were very worn, probably from eating the coarse bread and the grit!

Brewers made a thick beer from barley loaves that was very popular with people at all levels of society. In the inscriptions in some pyramids, the Pharaoh requests thousands of jugs of beer to be left for his spirit. Beer was easy and cheap to make, so poor farmers could add it to their meager diet. To make it, men standing in huge pottery jars trampled barley loaves into a mash with water. The mash was strained into another jar by a woman using a fiber basket. This jar was then sealed with a clay stopper.

Women shape loaves of bread and put them into a beehive-shaped oven while another woman makes the dough.

Men tread barley into beer mash.

The Egyptians, however, probably did not drink very much. One scribe wrote, "Do not indulge yourself in beer in case your speech becomes abusive. . . . If you collapse and hurt yourself, no one will help you . . . you are left lying on the ground."

Below: *Fishermen on papyrus skiffs with their catch*

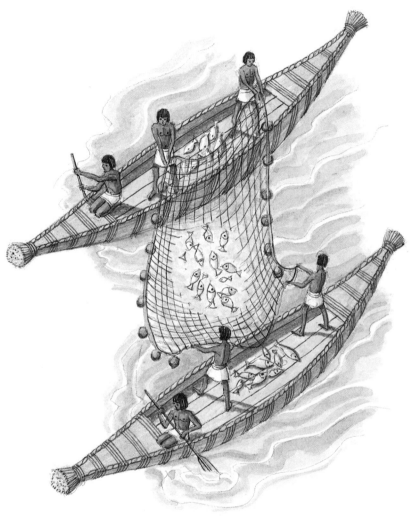

Wine was drunk only by people in the upper levels of Egyptian society. Bunches of grapes were gathered and taken to a trough over which a trellis had been constructed. Men clung to short ropes to avoid slipping and trod the grapes until the juice poured out through a funnel in the trough and was collected in jars.

Men cling to a trellis while they squash grapes for wine.

Beef was an important food for the Egyptians. They also ate geese, ducks, and fish, which they caught in the Nile. Fishermen on papyrus rafts set nets in the river. Many of them wore thick vest-like garments, possibly to keep them afloat if they fell into the river. Fish traps were also used. They were reed baskets with wide mouths and tapered ends. Other fishermen used a line. Large fish were gutted and cut up before being dried in the sun. Certain temples had rules forbidding priests to eat fish, probably because of a legend in which the body of the god Osiris was eaten by a fish.

TRADE AND COMMERCE

Accounts survive of lively market incidents which indicate that ordinary Egyptians gathered to trade goods with one another. For example, a man might have offered a well-made walking stick in exchange for some wheat. Another might have taken a vase in exchange for a pair of sandals, or a bowl for a basket of sycamore-figs. Tradesmen in the market usually dealt in household utensils and food, but more exotic things, even good-luck charms, were also available.

The bustle of crowds attracted thieves. Some robbers met their match in baboons that were trained to bite culprits.

Although there was no money, the value of goods was measured against a weight. A standard weight was called a *deben*. The weights were often shaped like a bull's head.

Tomb workers were paid with basic things such as beer or bread. Bonus payments were also given by the government. These would have been in special goods such as oil, salt, beef, or linen.

Trade with other countries was carried on by the Pharaoh and his top advisers. On one occasion a representative of the high priest of Amun was sent to Byblos to fetch

Among the bustle and canopies of a market town, cargoes of grain, beer, and linen are unloaded from the Nile. People will exchange manufactured goods like walking sticks or sandals for food and raw materials.

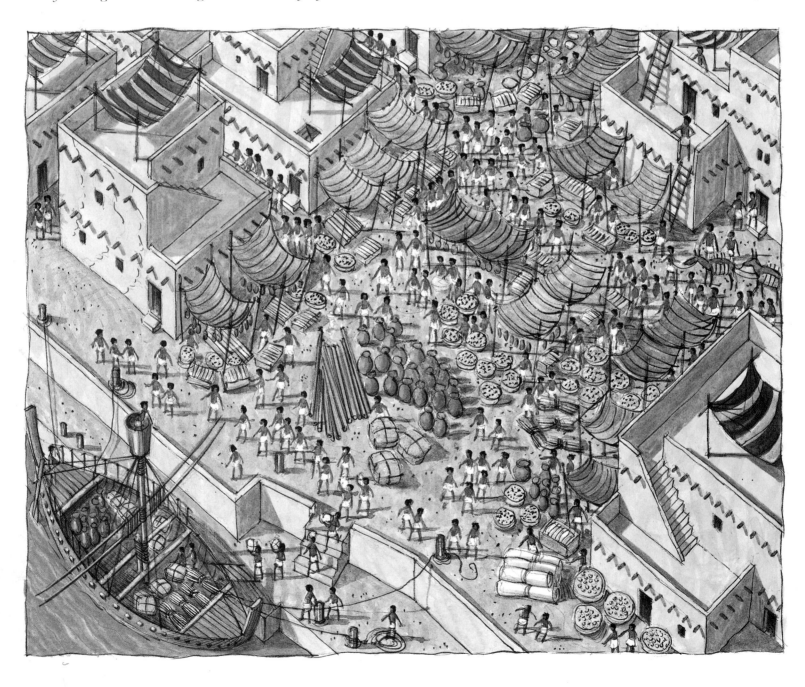

Boats sail on an expedition. They will return laden with African goods such as ivory, ostrich feathers, and gold, as well as animals.

timber for the boat of Amun. The prince of Byblos agreed to sell the cedar wood in exchange for five gold and five silver jars, ten royal linen garments, ten fine linen shawls, 500 linen mats, 500 cattle skins, 500 ropes, twenty sacks of lentils, and thirty baskets of fish.

Queen Hatshepsut sent an expedition of five ships down the Red Sea coast to the Horn of Africa to get frankincense. This came from special trees and was for use in the rituals of Amun-Re. Not only the gum but whole trees were transplanted to Egypt.

Another valued trade was in women cupbearers for the Pharaoh. King Amenhotep III wrote to a prince from the Middle East asking for thirty beautiful cupbearers who had "no deceit in their hearts." In exchange, the Pharaoh offered to send to the prince forty pieces of silver for each woman.

Eventually, Greek traders began to settle in Egypt in large numbers. They provided silver from their mines, olive oil, and the fine, painted pots in which the oil traveled. In return, they got flax to make linen sails, papyrus ropes for their boats, and wheat.

In the fourth century B.C., Egypt followed the rest of the Mediterranean countries and began to use coins as money.

MUMMIFICATION AND AFTERLIFE

Early burial in a desert pit

Present-day scientists studying a mummy

Duamutef (canopic jar)

Insety (canopic jar)

Ferrying the coffin to the desert cemetery

Praising Anubis, god of embalmers

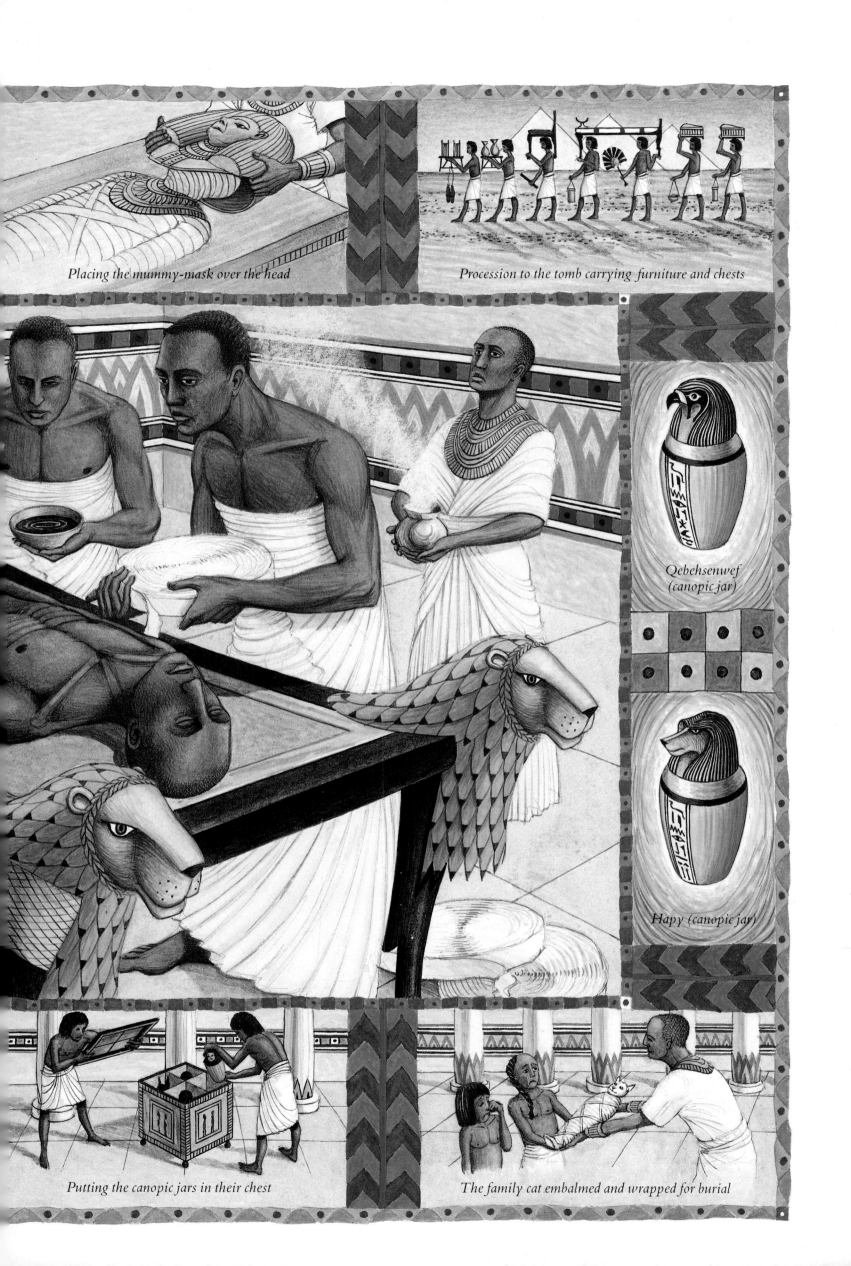

Placing the mummy-mask over the head

Procession to the tomb carrying furniture and chests

Qebehsenwef
(canopic jar)

Hapy (canopic jar)

Putting the canopic jars in their chest

The family cat embalmed and wrapped for burial

MAKING A MUMMY

The practice of mummification was a symbol of the Egyptians' desire to continue living in the next world once they had died.

In the earliest burials of ancient Egyptians, the body was put into a sleeping position, with the elbows and knees drawn together. A pit was dug in the sand, and the body was placed in it, along with useful things for the afterlife, such as jars of food. Sand was then thrown over the corpse. The body quickly dried and withered but did not decay. The dead person's spirit could then recognize the body and reenter it to bring it to life in the next world.

Gradually, the Egyptians discovered that these burials in the sand were being destroyed by jackals and hyenas who dug up the bodies and chewed them to pieces. The Egyptians then protected the bodies in coffins made of reeds or wooden planks. When the priests made reburials after tomb robbers had ransacked the graves, they found that the corpses were nothing but skeletons. The hot sand had been kept away from the flesh by the coffins so the bodies had decomposed leaving the spirits with no homes.

The Egyptians then developed a way to preserve the bodies by artificial means, called mummification. The development of this skill took hundreds of years. We know about the

Above: *Priests discover a grave looted by robbers after one of the early burials.*

Below: *Anubis, god of embalmers, performs a ritual over a mummified corpse. (From a painting on the wall of a courtier's tomb)*

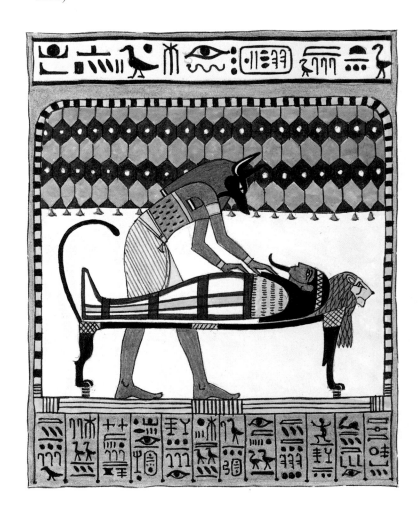

process from the ancient writers, from studies made of many mummies, and from experiments made on amputated human limbs.

A corpse was taken to the embalmers' pavilion. Embalmers, who were skilled craftsmen, put the body on an alabaster couch. The couch had a lion's head on each side of its front end.

First, the embalmers removed the organs. An incision was made in the lefthand side of the abdomen. Through it, the embalmers pulled out the intestines, the stomach, the liver, and the lungs. Only the heart was left in place. Since the brain was not considered to be the controlling center of the body, it was removed through the nose. The embalmers broke into the skull with chisels, chopped up the brain with hooks, and scooped it out of the head with spoons.

The embalmers had to dry out the flesh of the body to prevent it from rotting. They discovered that if the body was covered with a substance called crystals of natron, which was found in the Nile Valley, it would dry out within forty days. It would also be lifelike enough for the spirit to use.

The embalmers then rubbed ointment into the corpse, stuffed the internal cavities with dry materials so the body kept as full a shape as possible, and wrapped the limbs. The face was filled with packing to make the cheeks look full. The eyes were closed, or artificial eyes were inserted.

The body was then wrapped in linen bandages and returned to the relatives for burial. Four packages containing the insides that had been dried out in natron were also returned. Sometimes the wrapped-up body was smeared with a black resin to symbolize the life-giving Nile salt. This was described by Arab writers as pitch or "momia" — the origin of the word "mummy."

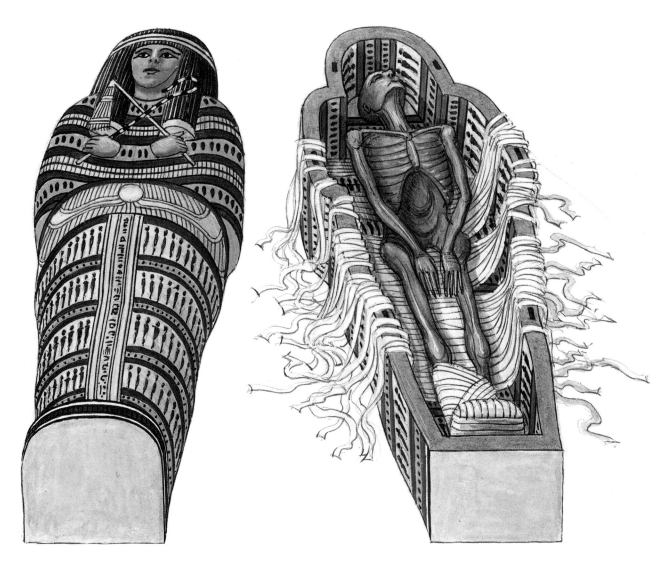

An embalmed body, with its wrappings removed, in its coffin covered with hieroglyphs and pictures of gods and goddesses

FUNERAL AND BURIAL RITUALS

Relatives of a dead official put the finishing touches on the arrangements that had already been made during his lifetime.

A gilded mask of linen stiffened with plaster was placed over the head and shoulders of the mummy. The body was decorated with funerary charms and put in an inner coffin that looked like a mummified corpse but that had free hands and an idealized face. This inner coffin might have been enclosed by two outer ones. The insides of the dead person were put into containers called canopic jars. The jars had stoppers in the shape of a god who protected the organs. The human-headed god Imsety guarded the liver; the baboon-headed god Hapy guarded the lungs; the jackal-headed god Duamutef guarded the stomach; and the hawk-headed god Qebehsenuef guarded the intestines. These gods were known as the sons of Horus. The four jars were then put into a canopic chest.

The corpse was taken across the Nile on a barge to the cemetery in the western desert. Women mourners were hired to accompany the coffin. They tore at their garments, threw sand over their hair, and wailed. As well as showing sorrow, this eerie sound was meant to scare away any evil being from the coffin. The coffin itself was carried on a boat-shaped sled protected by the eye of the hawk god Horus. Men pulled another sled behind carrying the canopic chest which often had the image of Anubis, the god of embalming and cemeteries.

At the tombside, the coffin was stood upright. A priest wearing the mask of Anubis supported it, and the closest female relative of the dead person knelt in front of it, crying. The important ceremony of Opening the Mouth then took place. Priests and the eldest son of the dead person scattered water over the coffin, burned incense, and touched the mouth of the mummy case with magical implements. One

A funerary procession makes its way from the Nile to the desert tomb. **Inset:** *Tutankhamun's funerary mask*

The Opening of the Mouth ritual is performed at the tomb side. (From a papyrus in the British Museum)

was a curved baton ending in a ram's head that suggested a constellation of stars. Another was an adze of iron, supposedly brought down from the sky. Spells were recited in which the god Ptah gave the dead person all the abilities of eating, speaking, and moving that he possessed when he was alive. At this point the dead person's spirit that had left the corpse during mummification returned into it. The corpse could be brought to life by the spirit in the burial chamber.

Other ceremonies then took place, such as the Muu dancers, who were men in tall conical crowns, performing an ancient ritual of the delta. There was also a sacrifice of some cattle or calves. The forelegs would be offered to the dead person and the remainder cooked and consumed by the guests at this funerary banquet. Any linen swabs or oils that had been used in the embalming were buried in a small pit near the tomb to prevent an enemy finding

them and casting a spell on the dead person.

The upper part of the tomb consisted of a chapel where the statues and paintings were situated. Mortuary priests and relatives could go there on anniversaries and festival days. The burial itself was at the bottom of a deep shaft sunk into the desert from either the tomb courtyard or the chapel. Along with the coffin were buried the canopic chest and valuables, such as caskets of jewelry, clothing, and items of furniture. In addition, a box of small figurines called *shabtis*, made from stone, wood, or glazed material, were included. The shabtis would answer the call of Osiris, god of the Underworld, and do any hard work that was necessary, such as digging irrigation canals. The belief in their magic was taken very seriously. Sometimes there was a shabti for every day of the year and overseer shabtis as well!

THE UNDERWORLD

The Egyptians believed that part of the soul stayed close to the burial chamber. These included the "ba," which had the head of the dead person but the body of a bird; the "ka," which was represented as the exact double of the person; the "shadow," and the "name." Another part of the spirit known as the "akh" went down through the floor of the burial chamber into the region called "Duat," or the Underworld.

The Egyptians believed in a host of perils that everyone had to overcome before reaching paradise. On the floor of some rectangular coffins, they painted the Book of the Two Ways. This was a map that showed the way through dangerous areas where there were lakes of fire or flame-spitting serpents. Often a papyrus was placed on the mummy or in a container nearby. This was a passport through hazardous regions. Egyptologists call it the Book of the Dead, but the ancient Egyptians called it the Book of Coming Out by Day. It was seen as a way of securing eternal life and the Egyptians gave it that name because they had a fear of being shut in darkness.

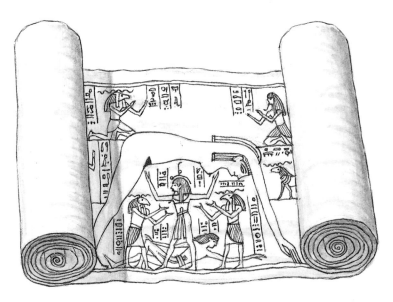

A Book of the Dead showing the sky goddess stretching her body across the Earth

In the Underworld, the soul had to get through gateways guarded by terrifying gods with heads of hippopotamuses, vultures, lions, and serpents. They guarded the gates to the realm of Osiris, and it was their task to prevent anyone unworthy from passing through. The Book of the Dead taught the soul the names of these fierce gods and gave it sufficient power to enter the gates in safety.

A selection of ferocious Underworld gods

In the Underworld, the heart of a dead person is weighed in the scales against the feather of the goddess of truth.

also showed the goddess called Devourer of the Dead beside the scales. She has the head of a crocodile, the body of a lioness, and the hind parts of a hippopotamus. If the heart were found guilty, it would be tossed to the Devourer of the Dead, who would instantly chew it up and swallow it. This act brought complete destruction on all parts of the soul and the person's afterlife. All the papyruses show the dead person being declared innocent of crimes by Thoth, god of wisdom, and passing into the throne room of Osiris.

The Egyptians imagined that the innocent person proceeded to a paradise that was the mirror of the Nile Valley but without any hardships. It was hoped that the whole family would be there together for eternity. The Egyptians called this paradise the Fields of Iaru.

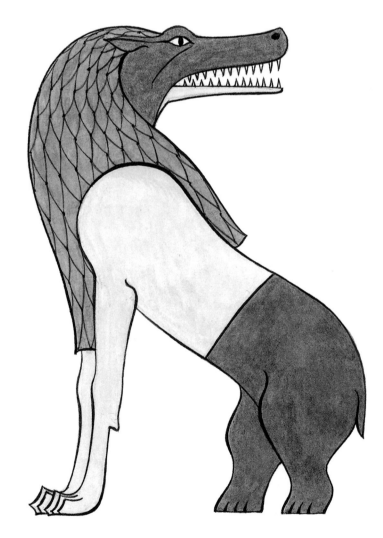

The goddess Ammut was made of a crocodile, lion, and hippopotamus. It was thought that she would chew up the heart of anyone who failed the truth test and so destroy their afterlife.

Finally, the soul reached the "Hall of the Two Truths," where it was judged to see if the dead person was fit to live forever in the kingdom of Osiris. A pair of scales was used for the judgment. The dead person's heart was put in one pan. In the other pan sat Maat, the goddess of truth, shown as a woman with a feather on her head. Forty-two gods then questioned the heart, accusing its owner of crimes such as murder, robbery, violence against children, and desecration of temple property. The heart would deny these charges, and the goddess of truth would determine if it was lying.

Naturally, the Egyptians hoped to pass this rigorous examination. They always depicted the heart as balanced against the goddess Maat and never weighed down with evils. But they

THE DISCOVERY OF ANCIENT EGYPT

Above: *Howard Carter gazes on Tutankhamun's coffin.*

For centuries the monuments of the Pharaohs were almost never seen by Western eyes. When Napoleon invaded Egypt in 1798, people in Europe began to hear about the vast tombs and temples and their decorations because scholars and artists accompanied the soldiers to record everything of interest in the country.

People began to go to Egypt to help with irrigation projects. One man, Giovanni Belzoni, hoped to make his fortune there. He was a large man and was famous as a circus strongman. When he got to Egypt, he turned his attention to the antiquities and obtained, for example, colossal statues of pharaohs and shipped them to Europe. His rough and ready approach to the monuments would be severely criticized today, especially since he once crushed many mummies when he fell over in a tomb in Thebes. But he did make some good discoveries. He was the first European to enter the magnificent 330-foot tomb of Seti I in the Valley of the Kings, the pyramid of Khafre at Giza, and the great temple of Ramses II at Abu Simbel.

Artists such as David Roberts visited the Nile Valley and produced wonderful

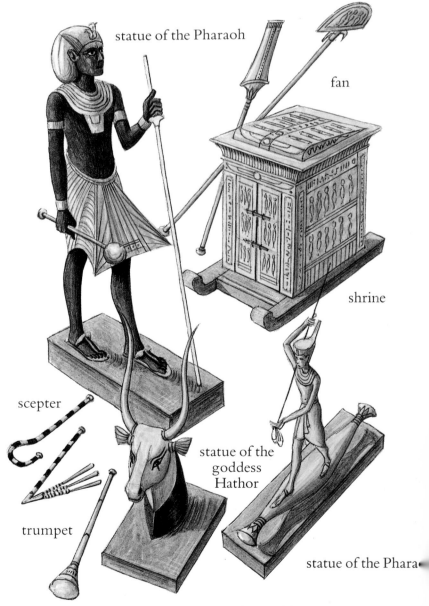

statue of the Pharaoh

fan

shrine

scepter

trumpet

statue of the goddess Hathor

statue of the Phara[...]

Above and opposite: *Treasures of Tutankhamun*

paintings of the most impressive tombs. Writers such as Amelia Edwards told of the grandeur of the monuments and her travels in Egypt in her book, *A Thousand Miles Up the Nile*. The mystery of how to read hieroglyphs was unraveled by a Frenchman, Champollion, who deciphered the code written on the Rosetta Stone, which had been discovered during Napoleon's campaign. It is now on display in the British Museum in London.

Instead of simply looting Egypt's treasures for European museums, archaeologists began to take a more responsible approach. The Frenchman Mariette, who made many important discoveries, was one of these people. He found the Serapeum at Saqqara, which contained the underground burial vaults for the sacred bulls of Memphis.

During the twentieth century, many spectacular finds have been made in the sands of Egypt. In 1922, Howard Carter discovered the virtually intact tomb of the young Pharaoh Tutankhamun. The 3,000 objects buried with him are still in the process of being properly studied. Later, Pierre Montet made some remarkable finds at Tanis, in the Nile Delta. Among the royal funerary equipment found were coffins of solid silver and a beautiful mask of the Pharaoh Psusennes.

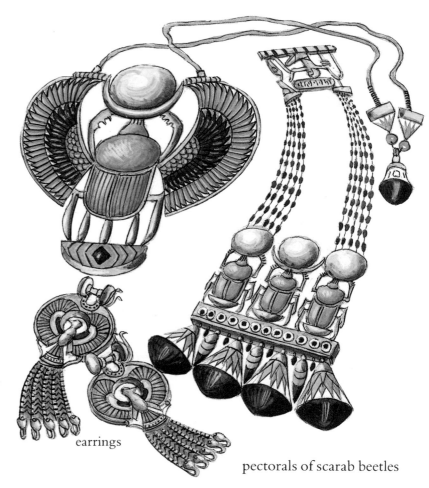

earrings

pectorals of scarab beetles

Egyptologists today are working on two different types of sites. The desert cemeteries such as Saqqara still provide splendid discoveries. Recently, a joint British and Dutch expedition has found the tomb of Horemheb, Tutankhamun's general and later Pharaoh himself; the tomb of Maya, treasurer for Tutankhamun; and the tomb of Princess Tia, sister of Ramses II.

Other archaeologists are rescuing as much information as possible about Memphis, the great political capital of Egypt, which has almost disappeared beneath silt and palm trees. Other towns, such as el-Asmounein, city for the temple of the god Thoth, and the workmen's village at Akhenaten's capital at el-Amarna, are being studied down to the very last detail. The discoveries from these less glamorous sites are as valuable in our understanding of Ancient Egypt as golden jewelry from a royal tomb.

There are spectacular discoveries still to be made. For example, where is the tomb of the high priest of Amun, Herihor? He ruled Upper Egypt as Pharaoh and must have had a burial among gold and jewels. The deserts and silt mounds of Egypt are far from giving up their last secrets about the civilization of the Pharaohs.

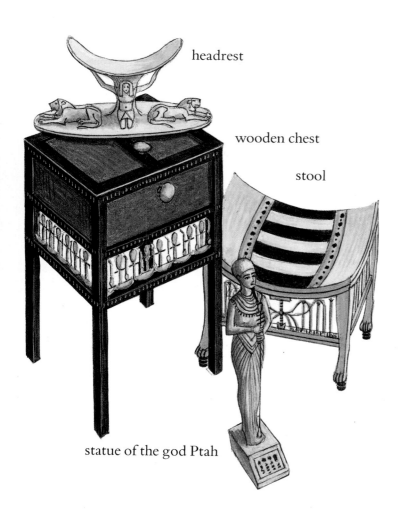

headrest

wooden chest

stool

statue of the god Ptah

TIME CHART

There is no way to know exactly when these events took place; even the experts disagree. The dates given here are those used by The British Museum.

EGYPT

B.C.

3000 **Unification of Upper and Lower Egypt**
Development of hieroglyphs

to 2575 **Early Dynasties**
Foundation of the capital, Memphis
Step pyramid built for King Djoser

to 2150 **Old Kingdom**
Great Pyramid of King Khufu built
Influence of the cult of Re, sun god of Heliopolis
Rise of worship of Osiris, god of the Underworld

to 2040 **First Intermediate Period**
No overall pharaoh but powerful princes rule in different regions

to 1640 **Middle Kingdom**
King Mentuhotep of Thebes reunites Egypt
King Senwosret III conquers Nubia and secures gold supply routes by building huge fortresses

to 1550 **Second Intermediate Period**
Foreign invaders called the Hyksos dominate Egypt from their capital Avaris in the northeast delta

to 1307 **New Kingdom: Dynasty XVIII**
King Ahmose of Thebes drives out the Hyksos
Rule of Queen Hatshepsut
King Tuthmosis III creates a vast empire
King Akhenaten and Queen Nefertiti promote worship of the sun god Aten and found new capital called "Horizon of the Sun Disk" at el-Amarna
On advice of senior ministers, King Tutankhamun, aged about eleven years, abandons el-Amarna and restores the traditional gods

to 1196 **New Kingdom: Dynasty XIX**
King Seti I builds beautiful temple to Osiris at Abydos
King Ramses II narrowly escapes defeat in the battle of Kadesh against the Hittites from Anatolia (modern Turkey)

THE REST OF THE WORLD

B.C.

c3000 New Stone Age in northern Europe

1800–1400 Stonehenge built in Britain
1650 Mycean civilization in Greece

1500–1300 Bronze Age in northern Europe

Queen Hatshepsut's temple

c1200 End of siege of Troy: the Greeks captur Troy by hiding in the wooden horse
(DYN XIX) Most likely time for events described in the Bible as the Exodus

Temples built at Abu Simbel
Great Hypostyle Hall built in the
temple of Karnak at Thebes, sacred
to Amun-Re

to 1070 **New Kingdom: Dynasty XX**
King Ramses III stops invasion of
Egypt by the sea peoples from the
Aegean and Asia Minor
Tomb workers in the Valley of the
Kings stage first recorded strike
Conspiracy in the royal harem to kill
King Ramses III fails, and the
traitors, including a queen and
prince, are executed
Show trial of tomb robbers in reign of
King Ramses IX

to 712 **Third Intermediate Period: Dynasty XXI**
New royal family in capital of Tanis
High priests of Amun-Re rule at
Thebes
Dynasty XXII
Descendants of Libyan princes
become pharaohs

to 657 **Nubian Dynasty XXV**
King Piye from Napata, in the Sudan,
conquers Egypt
Renovation of ruined temples
Assyrian army under King
Ashurbanipal conquers Egypt

to 525 **Saite Dynasty XXVI**
New royal family from Sais in the
delta
Persians invade Egypt
Dynasty XXX
Last independent Egyptian pharaohs
King Nekhtharheb driven out by
Persian army
Alexander the Great
332 Alexander liberates Egypt from
Persian rule
Foundation of Alexandria
323 Alexander dies at Babylon
304 General Ptolemy declares himself
Pharaoh

to 30 **Ptolemaic Dynasty**
Mark Antony and Egyptian Queen
Cleopatra lose the battle of Actium
Queen Cleopatra commits suicide
Octavian, later Emperor Augustus,
becomes master of Egypt

Temple of Nefertari at Abu Simbel

509 Founding of Roman Republic

44 Murder of Julius Caesar

INDEX